Thanks
for
Being My
FRIEND

The Riverboat Adventures

1. *Escape Into the Night*
2. *Race for Freedom*
3. *Midnight Rescue*
4. *The Swindler's Treasure*
5. *Mysterious Signal*
6. *The Fiddler's Secret*

Adventures of the Northwoods

1. *The Disappearing Stranger*
2. *The Hidden Message*
3. *The Creeping Shadows*
4. *The Vanishing Footprints*
5. *Trouble at Wild River*
6. *The Mysterious Hideaway*
7. *Grandpa's Stolen Treasure*
8. *The Runaway Clown*
9. *Mystery of the Missing Map*
10. *Disaster on Windy Hill*

Let's-Talk-About-It Stories for Kids

You're Worth More Than You Think!
Secrets of the Best Choice
You Are Wonderfully Made!
Thanks for Being My Friend

FOR ADULTS

Either Way, I Win: God's Hope for Difficult Times

LET'S TALK ABOUT IT
STORIES FOR Kids

Thanks for Being My FRIEND

LOIS WALFRID JOHNSON

BETHANY HOUSE PUBLISHERS
MINNEAPOLIS, MINNESOTA 55438

Thanks for Being My Friend
LET'S-TALK-ABOUT-IT STORIES FOR KIDS
Revised Edition 2000
Copyright © 1988, 2000
Lois Walfrid Johnson

Published by Bethany House Publishers
A Ministry of Bethany Fellowship International
11400 Hampshire Avenue South
Minneapolis, Minnesota 55438
www.bethanyhouse.com

Printed in the United States of America by
Bethany Press International, Minneapolis, Minnesota 55438

Library of Congress Cataloging-in-Publication Data

    Thanks for being my friend / by Lois Walfrid Johnson.
        p. cm. — (Let's talk about it stories for kids)
Summary: Brief stories and devotions examine the responsibilities,
problems, and pleasures of friendship.
    ISBN 1–55661–653–8 (pbk.)
    1. Friendship—Religious aspects—Christianity—Juvenile literature.
[1. Friendship. 2. Christian life. 3. Prayer books and devotions.]
I. Title.
BV4647.F7 J64 2000
241'.6762—dc21
                                         00–008381

*To every kid
who wants to know Jesus
as your forever Friend*

and especially to

*Jessica Lee
Daniel Jeffrey
Justin Kevin
Jennifer Christine
Nathaniel Kevin
Karin Lyn
and
Elise Grace*

LOIS WALFRID JOHNSON is the bestselling author of more than twenty-five books. Her work has been translated into twelve languages and has received many awards, including the Gold Medallion, the C. S. Lewis Silver Medal, the Wisconsin State Historical Society Award, and five Silver Angels from Excellence in Media. Yet Lois believes that one of her greatest rewards is knowing that readers enjoy her books.

In her fun times Lois likes to camp, bike, cross-country ski, be with family and friends, and talk with young people like you. Lois and her husband, Roy, live in Minnesota.

For more information about the author and her books, visit her Web site: LWJbooks.com

Contents

To the Kids Who Read This Book

"I wish I could be more popular with the other kids," said Kaitlin.

Do you have the same wish? Or do you think of it another way? "I'd like to be a sports hero, or a famous singer, or a space scientist."

Zachery was afraid to tell what he'd like to be. But he spent every spare minute throwing a football. Someday, maybe, he'd make the long pass that would win a big game. And wow! What a day that would be!

If you have those secret feelings, you have plenty of company. Most of us want people to think we're great. We want them to admire what we do and tell us we're totally awesome. Feeling that way can help you make good choices—to be more thoughtful of others, work hard to succeed, or choose right actions instead of wrong.

But when Kaitlin wanted to be popular and Zachery wanted to be a football hero, they were saying more: "I want to fulfill a dream, to be noticed, to have friends."

Friends come in all sizes and shapes. Some are young, some old, some just your age. Some are members of your family, grandparents or other relatives, neighbors, or pets.

Some are kids next door, at church, at school, or in your homeschooling group.

Friends are kids and grown-ups you know and love. They're people you have fun with and people who cry with you when you hurt.

The stories in this book are about kids who want friends and good relationships with others. But these kids don't always have it easy. Sometimes they're afraid or angry or mixed-up. Sometimes they feel that everyone else wins and they lose. Sometimes they think, *I don't have a single friend in the whole world!* Often they find that in their relationships they need to make life-changing choices.

The Bible tells about someone like that. Long ago Daniel was a prisoner of war living in Babylon. His king liked Daniel and wanted to make him ruler over the whole kingdom. But Daniel's enemies were jealous and plotted against him. They asked the king to issue a command that no one could pray to any god or man except him.

When the king listened to these evil men and gave that order, Daniel had to make a choice. Would he try to do what was popular? Would he do what his enemies wanted, even though it was wrong? Or would he choose God's side, in spite of the cost?

Daniel's life was at stake, but he didn't try to hide his choice. Praying meant so much to him that Daniel kept on, even though it was a matter of life or death. He didn't even huddle down in a closet. Instead, he threw open his windows toward Jerusalem. Three times a day he prayed to the Lord God of Israel, asking for help.

When his enemies told the king, Daniel was thrown into the lions' den. Can you imagine what a fearful place that would be? How those lions could roar and pounce upon their prey at any moment? How they could open their great mouths and chomp down on Daniel?

All through the long, dark night, those man-eating lions surrounded him. But in the morning, Daniel was unharmed. No wound was found on him because he trusted in his God!

The book of Daniel tells us, **"The people who know their God shall be strong and do great things"** (Daniel 11:32b, TLB). But Daniel didn't start trusting God when he landed in the den in front of those roaring lions. **Daniel knew God *before* the big test came.** He trusted God to close the mouths of the lions. Yet Daniel also believed that no matter what happened to him, God would be with him.

Daniel knew God as his friend, and you can also know God in that way. While on earth, Jesus told His disciples, "I have called you friends." What does it mean to be a friend of Jesus—to know Him as the greatest friend you have? What does it mean to have His help?

The stories in this book show kids who face the kind of problems you know about. These boys and girls need to make choices—whether to lose their battles or accept God's help and win. They need to decide if they'll become like Daniel—an in-spite-of-it kid with Holy Spirit power.

As you read the stories, put yourself in their gym shoes. Ask, "What would I do if this were happening to me or one of my friends?" Talk with your mom or dad, a teacher, or another special grown-up about the questions at the end of each story.

You'll see new ways of making choices. You'll think about how to deal with things that bother you. Then turn the book upside down. Repeat the Bible verse to yourself until you receive the help it gives. Say the prayer, or pray in your own words. Whenever you turn to God, you receive a power greater than your own.

You'll catch on to something big. **It's important to use the Bible in your choices. It's your laser sword against your enemies.** Often there's a story or verse that fits exactly what you need to know. Other times you need to think about the overall teaching of the Bible. For instance, Jesus tells us to love one another. If you wonder about doing something, ask yourself, "Would it *help* someone (show love)? Or would it *hurt* that person?"

In the choices you make, dare to think big and be like Daniel. But be honest with Jesus and tell Him right up front, "I need your help." Because you ask for His help, you'll get it.

You see, **Jesus wants to be your forever Friend. *Whoever* you are, He loves you. He stands with His arms open, ready to help you with whatever you face. With Him you can always say, *Thanks, Jesus, for being my Friend!***

Family
Christmas

"Can we cut our own Christmas tree this year?" asked Darren.

"That's a good idea!" Dad pushed aside his dinner plate. "When do you want to do it?"

"How about tomorrow afternoon? It's Saturday."

"Let me think," Dad said.

Darren felt sure that Dad didn't want to say it, but there would be football on TV. Dad really liked to watch.

Then Darren's older sister, Ashley, jumped in. "I want to go Christmas shopping with my friends tomorrow."

"I really need to bake Christmas cookies," Mom told them.

"And I wanna go ice-skating," said Darren's little brother, Riley.

"Hey, we never do stuff together anymore!" Darren exclaimed.

"Darren's right," said Dad. "How about it? I think we should go."

"Oh, Daaadd!" complained Ashley.

"No, I mean it," Dad said. "Every one of us will have to give up something, but won't it be worth it?"

Mom looked at him and smiled. "How about if everyone eats fewer cookies?"

Dad grinned, and Darren hoped Mom didn't really mean it. That would be awful.

Riley was the hardest to convince, but finally he said yes. The next afternoon everyone piled into the van. Even their golden Lab, Taffy, went along.

When they reached the Christmas tree farm, Darren snapped on Taffy's leash. Dad took a saw out of the back of the van. The man who owned the trees told them where to go, then left them on their own.

Once away from the buildings, Darren let Taffy go. Instantly the big dog shot after a rabbit. Watching Taffy bound through the snow, Darren felt as if he, too, were set free—let loose or something.

Dad looked around at each of them. "It feels good to be out in the woods with all of you."

Mom smiled and took Dad's hand. Riley trudged along behind, still mad that he hadn't been able to go skating. But Ashley seemed to have forgotten about shopping and talked with Darren.

When they reached the Christmas trees, the family found themselves alone. The young trees filled an open field on the edge of an older woods. As Darren watched, Taffy took off again. Soon he disappeared behind the huge trunk of a fallen tree.

"Okay, spread out!" said Dad. "Find the tree you like."

Each member of the family decided on something different. Riley discovered a scrawny little pine about his size. Mom wanted a fat one. "It'd be perfect near the living room window."

Dad thought they should go as tall as possible and set it

in the corner this year. And Ashley wanted a spruce instead of a pine.

Dad grinned. "Well, Darren, you haven't picked your favorite. Who's going to get first choice?"

"Let's have a snowball fight," said Darren. "The one who wins can pick."

Dad looked around for an open spot. "Okay, over there, where we won't hurt the trees."

"But no ice balls," Mom said quickly. "And you can't hit anyone in the head."

Darren claimed the huge tree trunk on the edge of the woods. By the time Dad signaled the beginning of the fight, Darren had a stockpile of snowballs.

Mom was the first one out, but she went laughing just the same. Riley was next. Taffy ran back and forth between snowballs.

Ashley and Dad wanted to join forces, but Darren wouldn't let them. It took a while, but finally he volleyed one snowball after another in their direction. Three hit Ashley almost at one time. Dad started laughing, and Darren got him, too.

"We surrender, we surrender!" Dad called out.

"Okay, Darren, it's your choice," Mom said.

Darren took a long time to make up his mind. It seemed he walked around every Christmas tree in the whole field. Finally he pointed out his choice.

"Why do you want that one?" Mom was curious.

Darren grinned. "It's a spruce for Ashley. And you see here? The backside is scrawny for Riley. It's tall for Dad and fat for Mom."

By now everyone was laughing, and Taffy barked along with them.

"And you, Darren? What do you want in a tree?" asked Dad.

Darren grinned again and didn't answer. If he had to tell them, he wasn't sure what he'd say. But one thing he did know—Christmas was off to a good start.

TO **TALK** ABOUT

▶ Sunday afternoon used to be a time when many families did something together. What are some reasons why it's harder for families to be together now?

▶ What did each person in Darren's family have to give up in order to pick out a Christmas tree?

▶ What is the difference between *finding* free time and *making* time for being together? In what ways does your family *make* time to do things together?

▶ Some families set aside Friday night for a special time together. Using their sleeping bags, they camp out in a room of their house. What special things does your family like to do together? What kinds of things do you do in different seasons of the year?

▶ If you don't have a family tradition of doing things together, in what ways can you start?

▶ How do special times help the members of your family laugh with each other and grow closer?

▶ What family stories do you share? Maybe they involve a time when something funny happened to one of you. Or maybe one of you said something so funny that the rest of you have never forgotten it. Each time you tell such stories they get bigger, and you start laughing before you even get the words out. **Think about your special family stories and remember them together whenever you can.**

If your mom and dad don't live together, what do you like to do when you're with your mom? When you're with your dad? What are your special family stories?

"The joy that the Lord gives you will make you strong." Nehemiah 8:10b (TEV)

Thank you, Lord, for special family times. Thanks for times when we giggle and laugh and do fun things together. Make us strong as a family, okay? Thanks, Jesus.

Camp Show-Off

Josh swung onto the upper bunk and lay down. From there he watched Nate, his camp counselor. When Nate wasn't looking, Josh slid into his sleeping bag with all his clothes still on.

He'd been at church camp for two days now. They hadn't been easy days. Already the camp director had gotten after Josh for throwing food in the dining hall. Even worse, Josh felt strange about being with these kids. Sure, he liked his counselor, Nate. And Pete and some of the other guys in his cabin were great.

But Josh wished he could belong—to be a real part of the group. Instead, he always felt at the edge of things. For some reason he needed to prove himself.

Now it haunted him. *I didn't mean to be rude to Pete, but I was*.

Earlier that day Pete had started talking about the neat things he and his dad did together. Next week after camp, the family would go on another trip.

Hearing about it, Josh blurted out, "Aw, my dad's got a better job than yours. He's gonna take me on a trip to Hawaii."

Pete looked kind of strange, but he didn't say anything.

He didn't say anything more about his own family, either.

Maybe he knows I only see Dad once a year, Josh thought. *Maybe he knows Dad really won't take me to Hawaii.*

Suddenly Josh felt ashamed about his lie and trying to look good. *I didn't mean to put down Pete.* At the same time he thought, *I'll show 'em. I'll get 'em to notice me.* Feeling pleased with himself, Josh remembered the plans he had made.

"Good night, you guys!" Nate called as he turned out the lights.

Josh lay in the darkness, going through his plans step by step. *All I've gotta do is wait until everyone's asleep.*

The minutes ticked away, and Josh grew restless. The other boys talked and joked and finally grew quiet. At last Josh dared to lean down from his upper bunk. When he peered into the dim light of the cabin, everyone, including Nate, seemed asleep.

Slowly, carefully, Josh climbed down and tiptoed across the room. He even managed to open and close the door without making it squeak. Once outside, he hurried to the place under the cabin where he'd hidden the things he collected.

It took two trips to bring all of it up near the dining hall. Once there, Josh stepped into the flower bed, stood a long, pointed pole upright, and pushed it into the dirt. Taking shorter poles and a rope, he tied two crosspieces into an X. Then he tied the X onto the tall pole.

A yard light gave just enough of a glow for Josh to see how it looked. Standing back to view his work, he felt good. *Yup, it'll make a great scarecrow.*

Using jeans for legs and a shirt for arms, he stuffed them with crumpled newspapers he'd found in the trash bin. Then came his masterpiece. Working quickly, Josh filled a pillow-case with more newspapers. With another piece of rope he tied the head in place.

Once again Josh stood back. Even in the dim light he saw the face he'd drawn on the pillowcase. Dark hair, glaring eyes, mustache, beard, and a mouth that turned down in a scowl. The face closely resembled Mr. Fleming, the camp director.

Josh grinned. *Just how he looked when he was mad at me.*

The next morning the whole camp buzzed. When the rumor started that Josh had done it, he felt good. But no one could prove anything. By afternoon Josh wished he had left just one clue so he could get credit.

At supper Josh caught his counselor watching him from across the table. There was something in Nate's eyes that Josh didn't like. *Can he see right through me?* Josh wondered.

When Thursday night came, everyone gathered at the beach for the closing campfire. Josh sat on the outer edge of the circle, feeling as alone as he had all week. *What a bunch of junk they're dishing out*, he thought. *This Jesus—what a friend He'd be.*

Then Josh's heart started to pound, as though it were going to beat right out of his chest. Nate was speaking to the whole group that night, but he seemed to be talking right to Josh.

"Are you lonely?" Nate asked. "There's no one who can fill every space in your heart except Jesus. Are you afraid no one will notice you? Do you lie and show off to get attention? Do you feel like you want to belong, but you're afraid to try? There's someone you need more than anyone. It's Jesus."

Deep inside, Josh felt like he was crying and couldn't stop. *Sissy stuff*, he thought. *I'm not gonna cry for anything*.

Trying to push down his feelings, Josh thought about leaving. He wanted to run away from the quiet voice telling him about Jesus. He didn't want to be honest in front of the kids. He didn't want to be honest about how uncomfortable he felt. Most of all, he didn't want to be honest with himself.

But Nate kept talking. "Jesus loves you so much that He died on the cross for you. He died to take away your sin. He wants to forgive you. All you have to do is ask Him."

Suddenly Josh couldn't hold in all of his mixed-up feelings. He began sobbing and couldn't stop. All the loneliness he'd felt, all the bragging and asking for attention, all the feelings of not fitting in overwhelmed him.

When Nate finished speaking, Josh moved closer to the campfire. *I don't want to tell him what's wrong*, Josh thought. But when he did, Nate told Josh what to do.

"Sin—doing wrong things—separates you from Jesus," Nate explained.

With Nate's help, Josh prayed, asking Jesus to forgive him.

When that was taken care of, Josh invited Jesus into his life. "Jesus, I ask you to be my Savior and Lord," Josh prayed, the way Nate had told him to.

In that moment a great weight fell away from Josh. He drew a deep breath, hardly able to believe it himself. *Jesus loves me*, he thought. *Jesus really loves me!*

Inside, Josh knew that Jesus is real.

TO **TALK** ABOUT

▸ Josh wanted to be loved and accepted by the other kids. Even if he knew that he belonged, would that take care of all of his emptiness? Why or why not?

▸ Josh learned that Jesus loved him in spite of the things he had done. Talk about Romans 5:8: "But God has shown us how much he loves us—it was while we were still sinners that Christ died for us!" (TEV). What does this verse mean?

▸ Why is Jesus the only person able to fill the emptiness Josh felt? Some more clues: "If you confess that Jesus is Lord and believe that God raised him from death, you will be saved. For it is by our faith that we are put right with God; it is by our confession that we are saved" (Romans 10:9–10 TEV). To confess something means to say with your mouth what you believe. Why is Jesus the only person who can help *you* with every need?

▸ Josh felt different after he confessed his sin, asked forgiveness, and invited Jesus into his life. But what if Josh *didn't* feel anything? Would he still be a Christian? Why or why not? Check out Romans 10:13: "Everyone who calls out to the Lord for help will be saved" (TEV). What does *everyone* mean?

▸ Do you know for sure that Jesus is your Savior and Lord? If not, what choice do you need to make?

If you'd like to invite Jesus into your life, you can pray these words:

> "Thank you, Jesus, for loving me so much that you died on the cross for me. I'm sorry about my sins and ask you to forgive me. I ask you to be my Savior and Lord. Thank you for your salvation."

The Bible promises that "whoever believes in the Son

has eternal life" (John 3:36a). If you have asked for forgiveness for your sin and asked Jesus to be your Lord and Savior, you have eternal life—a life with Jesus on earth and in heaven forever. It begins right now!

"God has given us eternal life, and this life has its source in his Son. Whoever has the Son has this life; whoever does not have the Son of God does not have life. I am writing this to you so that you may know that you have eternal life—you that believe in the Son of God." 1 John 5:11–13 (TEV)

Find and underline the word whoever in these two verses. Then underline the word *know*.

In the space below write down what you believe about Jesus' being your Savior and Lord.

It's Not Fair!

Lexee was angry when she came to the supper table. Partway through the meal, she started in. "You always let Brianna do what she wants. Why does she get to go to the volleyball tournament, and I don't?"

"She's older than you," Dad said. "When you're Brianna's age, you'll get to do the things she's doing now."

But Lexee wasn't satisfied. "You and Mom treat her differently than you treat me. And you treat Ethan differently, too. No matter what he does, you think it's cute."

Dad sighed. "Lexee, you know that Brianna is four years older than you, and Ethan is five years younger. We can't possibly treat you all the same."

"It's not fair!" said Lexee. "I think you *should* treat us all the same."

"Do you really?" asked Dad. "Do you want a baby-sitter like Ethan has when we go out?"

"Well, no," said Lexee. "But he always gets the prize in the cereal box."

Dad laughed. "Are you sure you want those prizes? A lot of them are for four- or five-year-olds. Or do you want the prizes because Ethan wants them?"

"Just the same, it's not fair!"

"Some things aren't fair," Dad said. "Sometimes we need to treat each of you differently. It's not because we love one of you more than another. We try to do what's best for each of you."

For a moment Lexee was quiet. *Is that really true?* she wondered. *Do Dad and Mom really try to do what's best for each of us?*

Mom broke into her thoughts. "How many for apple pie? There's a little bit left over from last night."

Everyone was too full, except for Brianna and Lexee. "I'll cut it," Lexee said. "Brianna always takes more than her share."

"Go ahead," said Mom. "You cut it, but then Brianna gets first choice."

Lexee groaned, making sure everyone heard. Ever since Lexee was a little kid, she had hated that family rule. If she didn't cut something even, she never got a chance to have the biggest piece.

While eating her pie, Lexee started thinking again. *Do Mom and Dad really love me as much as Brianna and Ethan? They always seem to get more attention. They always get the best.*

Just then the phone rang. Brianna jumped up. When she returned to the table, her face glowed. "David said he'd give me and some other kids a ride to the game. Okay?"

Mom looked at Dad. "Okay," they said, almost together.

A minute later Brianna was back. "I need to leave in twenty minutes. Can I be excused to get ready?"

Lexee exploded. "It's her turn to do dishes!"

"I know it is," said Brianna. "Can you help me out?"

"That's just what I've been talking about. You always get to do stuff I can't do!"

"How about trading with me?" Brianna asked. "I'll do one of your nights next week. Okay?"

Lexee sighed. "Nope. If I do dishes tonight, you work two nights for me next week."

"Uh, uh, uh," said Dad. "That's not fair to Brianna."

Lexee looked at Dad. He was right, of course. It wasn't fair. Much as she wanted to take advantage of Brianna, she'd better not—at least not in front of Mom and Dad.

"Okaaay." Lexee's voice told all of them how unhappy she was with the deal. "I'll do 'em tonight."

Brianna hugged her. "I'll tell you everything about the game when I get home!"

It seemed forever before Lexee finished the dishes. As she put away the leftover food, she felt angry. As she loaded the glasses and silverware into the dishwasher, she felt angry. No matter what Dad said, she still felt Brianna and Ethan got the best end of every deal.

But then as she rinsed off the plates, Lexee remembered something—a time when Brianna had helped her out. One of Brianna's friends had three tickets for the ice-skating show, and Brianna got Lexee invited.

As she scrubbed the pots and pans, Lexee remembered something else. Once, she got to go to the circus with Ethan and his friends. Sure, they were younger, but it was still fun.

By the time Lexee wiped off the table and counter, she felt a bit better inside.

She'd been sleeping a couple of hours when her sister crept into their bedroom. As Brianna stumbled over the clothes on the floor, she crashed into a chair. Lexee woke up.

When she moaned, Brianna exclaimed, "Oh, I'm so glad you're awake! I want to tell you everything we did." Brianna turned on the light.

Rubbing the sleep out of her eyes, Lexee rolled over and stuffed a pillow under her head.

Brianna's face still glowed. "It's so awesome to have fun with a bunch of kids who like the same things I do. They even *believe* the same things I do! Thanks for doing the dishes so I could get ready."

As Brianna dropped down on her bed, Lexee felt the cold outside air still clinging to her sister's clothes. But inside Lexee felt warm. For the first time in many weeks, she wanted to hear what Brianna had to say.

TO **TALK** ABOUT

▶ What is a happy family? Is it one where there are never disagreements? Or one where everyone knows it's okay to talk about what bothers them? Why do you think so?

▶ Why is it important that Lexee talked about how she felt? Do you agree or disagree with the answers Dad gave? Why?

▶ What does it mean to compete? Lexee was competing for something. What was it? What feeling made her want to compete?

▶ In some families everyone competes with everyone else. In others, members of the family try to cooperate. What does it mean to cooperate? How did Lexee and Brianna work together?

▶ Which kind of family is stronger—the one where everyone competes with each other or the one where family members cooperate? Why? In what ways does your family work together to do something fun or reach a goal?

▶ Lexee is a middle child. Sometimes a middle child wants to keep up with what an older brother or sister does. At the same time that middle child might feel pushed because a younger brother or sister can do something better. How can birth order make a difference in your life? If you have siblings, what things are special in your life because of the order in which you were born?

▶ If your father or mother does not live with you, the rules for that house may be different from the house where you live most of the time. Yet you still need to know how to cooperate. How can you work together when you go there?

▶ **When Jesus walked here on earth, He showed us how much He loves every person as an individual**. You, too, can help each person in your family feel they are special. How can you show a sister, brother, or parent that you love and value them the way they are? In what practical ways can you show your love?

Don't just think about your own affairs, but be interested in others, too, and in what they are doing. Philippians 2:4 (TLB)

Jesus, I'm used to looking out for Number One—and that's me. But I want to think more about others. Help me learn how to cooperate with the members of my family. Help me care about them and show them how special they are.

The Old Bike Trail

Shane felt glad that someday his teeth would look better. Yet for now he hated wearing braces.

"When we're done, you'll have a nice smile," the orthodontist told him.

Someday, thought Shane. Someday seemed like forever. It was years away. This morning was *now*—his first Sunday school class after getting braces. The bands and wires seemed to fill his entire mouth.

To make matters worse, a new girl joined their class that day. *Darcy looks like fun*, Shane thought. But then he wondered, *What will she think of the way I look?* Leaning his elbow on the table, he covered his mouth with his hand.

The first time his teacher called on him, Shane was still thinking about his braces.

"Shane," said Mrs. Jefferson again.

As though just waking up, Shane jumped. Everyone laughed.

When he tried to answer, Mrs. Jefferson stopped him. "I'm sorry, Shane, but I can't hear you. Why don't you take your hand away from your mouth? It'll help us understand what you're saying."

The boy next to Shane snickered, and everyone turned

in his direction. Now Shane felt as if he were one inch high. Heads and eyes seemed to tower above him, looking down to see his braces. Shane felt the warm flush of embarrassment come into his face. His tongue refused to move, and every thought flew out of his head. For the rest of the hour, Shane felt miserable.

As class ended, Mrs. Jefferson reminded them to bring their bicycles for their picnic the following Saturday. "Meet here at church at ten o'clock and bring a bag lunch. We'll take the old trail to the park."

The class had biked together once before. Shane remembered having a good time and looked forward to this trip. But now he didn't feel too sure about it.

When Shane woke up on Saturday, he still felt uncomfortable about his braces. As he pedaled into the church parking lot, he saw Darcy laughing with the other kids. Skidding to a stop, he pulled alongside.

"Hi, Shane!" the kids called out. Darcy even remembered his name. But when Shane said hi back, he thought of his braces and remembered not to smile. He caught Darcy's quick look and turned his head away.

Getting off his bike, Shane pretended he needed to check his tires. When he looked up, he saw Darcy watching. She started to smile, but again Shane turned away.

Soon all the kids were there and ready to leave. "I'll take the lead," Mrs. Jefferson said. "Will you go last, Shane? Just make sure everyone gets along okay."

While the kids fell into line, Shane waited. Those who knew each other best went first. Darcy pulled into line just ahead of Shane.

Except for a few places with loose gravel, the packed dirt of the trail made biking easy. Winding between trees, the path followed the twisting banks of a creek.

As time went on, the morning breeze died down and the sun grew warm. Now and then the bikers pedaled hard to conquer a hill, but going down the other side made up for it.

Spacing himself, Shane held back so he could swoop down the hills. As he came to the top of a rise, he heard a yell. Looking ahead, he saw Darcy lying at the bottom in a heap, her legs and arms tangled with her bike.

Shane soon reached her. Dirt smudged her face, and she looked shaky and scared.

"Hey! Wow! You really wiped out!" Shane knelt on the ground beside her. "Are you okay?"

Darcy nodded. "I mean, not really, but yeah." Her mouth turned up, and she tried to smile but didn't make it. Instead, she looked ready to cry.

Shane started to move her bike away. As he helped her sit up, Darcy winced.

"I'm sorry!" Shane said. "Where does it hurt?'"

Then he saw the gravel ground into her skinned knees. "Ouch!" he exclaimed. "When you wipe out, you do it big."

This time the smile reached Darcy's eyes.

Shane kept talking, trying to make her feel better. In a few minutes, Darcy stood up and managed to get back on her bike.

They took the rest of the trail at a slow pace. Just before they caught up to the others, Darcy smiled shyly. "I thought you didn't want to be friends with anyone. You never smiled."

My braces! Shane thought. *I forgot all about them!* But it didn't matter anymore. He and Darcy were friends now.

TO TALK ABOUT

▸ How did Shane act whenever he thought about his braces? What happened when he forgot about them?

▸ What do you suppose Darcy thought about Shane's braces?

▸ How did thinking about himself keep Shane from making a new friend?

▸ If you feel shy about making friends, it helps to ask other people questions about things they like to do. When they begin talking, you forget about yourself. What are some questions to ask a kid you've just met?

Jesus longs to be your forever Friend. How do you think He feels about things like braces or some other way you don't like your appearance?

Encourage one another and help one another, just as you are now doing. 1 Thessalonians 5:11 (TEV)

Thank you, Jesus, that things like braces don't last forever! Help me forget the things I can't change and think about how others feel. Thanks for the new friends you are going to give me!

Saturday Morning Car Wash

One evening Shannon and the kids in the neighborhood started talking about how to raise money. Kelly, one of the girls living down the block, needed a kidney transplant. Her family needed money for medical bills.

Shannon took charge. She liked organizing things and asked for ideas on what to do. "We could have a pancake supper," she suggested. "Our moms and dads would help."

"How about a carnival?" asked a boy. "We could bring things for prizes or stuff we could sell—like toys we don't use anymore."

After a lot of talk, they decided to hold a car wash on a Saturday morning two weeks away.

"My dad will let us have it in the parking lot of his office," said Shannon's best friend, Elise. "It's on a busy corner where lots of people will see us."

"Great!" Shannon exclaimed. "Let's make a list of what we need. First, someone for publicity. Who's good at making flyers?"

"I am," said Elise. "And I'll take 'em to all the stores around here."

"How about a notice in the bulletin of churches in the neighborhood?"

Someone else volunteered.

"Rags and buckets?"

Three boys offered to bring those.

"Car wax?"

A fourth boy said he'd try for a discount at a nearby store.

"Well, that's just about it," said Shannon. Then as the group started to break up, she remembered one more thing. "We'll need two long hoses or three shorter ones to reach from the outside faucet to the parking lot."

"I'll bring them," said D. R. "We've got two long hoses."

"Terrific," answered Shannon. "Now, does everyone know what they're supposed to do?"

Picking up the list, she read off each person's job. "Then we're all set. Talk about the car wash wherever you are. The more customers we get, the more money we'll make for Kelly. And everyone be there at eight-forty-five, ready to work."

The Saturday of the car wash dawned warm and sunny. As the kids gathered at the parking lot, Shannon knew the girls had done a great job on publicity. Wherever she had been the last few days, people had promised they'd show up. Now, fifteen minutes before the car wash was to start, Shannon checked to be sure they had everything.

"Buckets? Rags? Wax? Yup. And plenty of kids to help." Shannon was pleased.

But the next moment she felt a jolt. "Where's D. R. with the two hoses?"

No one had seen him that morning. Shannon's heart started to pound. "Uh-oh, are we in trouble?"

"I'll go call," Elise said. But the office building was locked. The nearest outside phone was a block away.

Just then their first customer drove in. A moment later three other cars lined up behind the first. Shannon looked at them, glad for the business. "But oh, wow! How can we keep up without a hose?"

She sent three of the boys with buckets to the faucet. But the cars were too dirty. Soon muddy brown water filled each bucket.

Shannon felt frantic. "We're gonna lose customers," she said and tried to set up a bucket brigade.

She was right. The driver of the third car gave a quick beep. Shannon went over to explain what was wrong. He pulled out of line and drove off.

The driver of the fourth car got out. "Hey, what's the trouble? Can I help?"

Shannon felt relieved when she recognized Mr. Wong, a man from her church.

"I've got two short hoses," he said. "I live three miles from here, but I'll see what else I can round up." He jumped back in his car and drove away.

Just then another driver pulled in. When Shannon explained, the woman said, "Sorry, I wanted to help out. But I can't wait around all day."

The man in the next car felt the same way and left.

Shannon didn't blame them, but she felt more angry every minute. Each customer they lost meant less money for Kelly. "All that publicity wasted!"

But Shannon also felt embarrassed. It hurt to plan something and not have it work. "I wonder if people think it's my fault." She dreaded seeing another customer—someone who'd think she didn't know what she was doing.

Just then D. R. rode up on his bike. Shannon pounced on him. "Where are the hoses?"

"Hoses?" D. R. looked blank, then remembered. "Ohhh. I forgot."

"You *forgot*?" Shannon asked. "The whole car wash depended on you, and you *forgot*?"

She couldn't remember ever being so angry. Picking up a bucket, she dumped the muddy water over D. R.'s head. "You take the world's prize for messing things up!"

As D. R. sputtered, Shannon picked up another bucket and stomped over to a waiting car. The moment she reached the driver, she turned on a smile, but inside she burned with anger. *How long before Mr. Wong comes back?*

TO **TALK** ABOUT

▸ **Being responsible means being someone other people can count on.** How did everyone except D. R. accept responsibility?

▸ What does it mean to say, "A chain is only as strong as its weakest link"? Who was the weakest link? How did all the kids suffer because he forgot his part?

▸ Why was it important that Shannon told D. R. how she felt?

▸ Did Shannon have a right to be angry about the hoses? Did she show her anger in the right way? Give reasons for your answers.

▸ When was Jesus angry about things people did? Check Mark 3:1–5 and John 2:13–17 for big clues. Do these verses mean Shannon has a right to be angry whenever she feels like it? Why or why not?

▸ Does Shannon have a right to hold a grudge toward D. R.? Why or why not?

▸ When the car wash is over and Shannon cools down, she needs to talk more with D. R. What do you think she should say about how she feels?

▸ If Shannon says, "I'm upset because we didn't have the hoses when we needed them," what could D. R. do to set things right? If you were D. R., what would you like to do about the money that's been lost?

▸ What are some things that make you angry? What are some ways you can deal with your anger?

▸ When Peter denied his relationship with Him, Jesus could have held a grudge and stayed hurt and angry. Check out John 18:17, 25–27. How did Jesus make sure that Peter knew things were okay between them? See John 21:15–17. What words did Jesus use?

If someone has done you wrong, do not repay him with a wrong. Try to do what everyone considers to be good. Romans 12:17 (TEV)

Jesus, when I feel upset, help me handle my anger in the right way. Help me talk to the person I have a problem with. Help us figure out what to do and put the problem behind us.

The Long Bus Ride

Antonio rolled onto his stomach and pulled the blankets over his head. Even so, he could hear Mama's voice.

"An-tone-ee-ohh! Time to get up!"

Antonio groaned and fell back to sleep. He woke to Mama's hand on his shoulder. "Wake up! Wake up! You'll miss your bus!"

Slowly his eyes came open. Rubbing them, Antonio yawned. He didn't like getting up in the morning. He'd much rather stay up nights and sleep late.

When Antonio finally sat up, Mama left the room. *Friday*, he thought with relief. *Well, at least tomorrow's Saturday. No school.*

But then Antonio thought about the day's long bus ride to school, and his stomach muscles tightened.

Forty-five minutes later he climbed aboard. This was the moment he dreaded, and there was no way to get around it.

"Tony!" Kurt called out from the back of the bus. "Sit here!"

Antonio shook his head and looked for a seat near the front.

"What's the matter, Tony? You runnin' scared or something?" yelled another boy. "We saved you a place."

This time Antonio forced a smile and answered. If he didn't they'd be after him the whole ride. "Nah, I like the scenery up here."

Dropping into an empty seat, he faced the front and pretended he didn't hear the answer. But on the inside Antonio hurt.

Will they ever stop? he wondered. *Every morning, every afternoon, it's the same old thing!*

The boys who usually got in trouble sat in the back of the bus. When school started that fall, Antonio sat with them. Then one day they started passing drugs. Antonio decided he'd had enough.

The next morning he sat farther forward in the bus. Since then the kids hadn't let up.

I know I'm right, Antonio told himself. *But it sure is hard sticking to what I believe.*

Most of the kids sitting near the front were much younger than Antonio. He felt almost as uncomfortable with them as with the boys at the back.

Once again Kurt called to him. Others joined in. Trying to pretend he didn't hear, Antonio stared out the window.

I'll beat 'em at their own game, he promised himself. *Who cares about them? I can make it on my own.* Yet Antonio wasn't sure he meant it.

As the bus stopped in front of school, Antonio stood up, eager to get away from the other boys. But Kurt pushed forward, past the place where Antonio stood between the seats. Turning around, Kurt blocked the aisle and turned his coldest stare on Antonio.

Being careful to stay far enough back so Kurt couldn't kick him, Antonio stepped into the aisle. Whatever Kurt did, it was always sneaky so the bus driver couldn't see.

But then as Antonio waited for the aisle to clear, Kurt's best friend moved up behind Antonio. Instantly every warning signal inside Antonio blinked red. Cold shivers ran down his spine as he wondered what they planned to do.

Antonio knew he could fight. He had done it before, and he was strong. But he'd be taking on more than Kurt, and Antonio felt scared. He couldn't possibly fight them all.

In that split second he faced the truth. *I can't do it alone. If they beat me up again, I might give in.*

Antonio hated the idea. He didn't want the guys to win. At the same time he felt afraid. So afraid that he silently prayed three words: *Help me, Jesus.*

In the next moment, something changed inside Antonio. Though short for his age, he straightened to his full height and stood his tallest.

Outwardly everything seemed the same. Kurt still stared at Antonio. He and his friend still hemmed Antonio in. But now Antonio had an idea about what to do.

Just then the bus driver saw Kurt in the mirror and called out, "Get moving, Kurt!"

All weekend long, Antonio thought about what to do. On Monday morning he got up before his mother called him. No matter how much he wanted to sleep, he turned on his light.

There, where no one could see what he was doing, he took out his Bible. "Help me, Jesus," he prayed. "Just help me get through the day."

Antonio began to read. It was strange how much better he felt after just a few verses. Then, as he prayed, the idea he'd had before came back. But up until now he'd always told himself NO!

No longer did Antonio tell himself he didn't need help. Instead, he knew that he did.

That morning at breakfast, Antonio told his mother about his long bus rides.

TO **TALK** ABOUT

▸ What important choices did Antonio make?

▸ What is the difference between saying NO! as if you mean it, and saying no as though you're half scared? Give an example. Why do tough kids pick on kids who seem scared?

▸ In what ways have you had to say NO! to other kids? What happened when you did?

▸ Praying about something is important, but it's also important to know when to ask for help. What's the difference between squealing on someone and asking for help? How can Antonio's mother help him without other kids knowing about it?

▸ **When you're afraid of what someone is doing to you, it's time to talk about it with the right person. That person can help you find a way to change what is happening to you.** Who are some people at school Antonio could have talked to about what was happening on the bus?

▸ Antonio started reading his Bible because he had a big need. If you're like Antonio, it helps to pray, "Jesus, what do you want me to know about. . . ?" (Tell Jesus what your special need is.) Begin reading in the Bible and stop when a verse seems real because it fits what's happening to you right now. **If you read the Bible every day, you'll know when the Holy Spirit is speaking to you. Words seem to jump off the page or there seems to**

----

be a big spotlight on them.

▸ Have you had times when the Bible seemed very real to you? What happened? Is there a verse that helped you face something hard? What is it?

▸ If you don't have a Bible, ask your mom or dad, or some-one else who can give you one. If you haven't read the Bible before, a good place to start is with the Gospel of John, the fourth book in the New Testament. Look in the contents at the beginning of the Bible, and you'll find it.

▸ **The Bible gives you a way to get to know Jesus. Remember? He wants to be your best Friend. Your always-with-you, forever Friend.**

Moses answered, "Don't be afraid! Stand your ground, and you will see what the Lord will do to save you today." Exodus 14:13 (TEV)

Jesus, I'm afraid. Show me what to do about the things that make me scared. Help me to be strong and not give in to wrong things. Then help me talk with a grown-up who will find a way to change what is happening to me.

Wedding in the Family

With a final look in the mirror, Jill pushed back a strand of her blond hair. Then she lined up at the back of the church with her sisters Hannah and Morgan.

As the shortest bridesmaid, she would lead the others down the aisle. The youngest of the four girls in their family, Jill often felt like a tagalong. Too old to be a flower girl, but much younger than her sisters, Jill had wondered if she'd be in the wedding. But when her sister Kelsey became engaged, she settled the problem.

"When I marry Adam, I want you with us," she said. "You're my junior bridesmaid! Okay?"

From that day on, Jill felt excited just thinking about the big moment of the wedding. At the same time, she wished she were as grown-up and attractive as her older sisters.

Nervously Jill touched the soft folds of her long blue dress. When she shifted her bouquet from one hand to the other, she saw that every church pew was filled. Suddenly the aisle seemed to stretch out forever.

Just then Hannah leaned forward to tell Jill that she looked great. But Jill felt sure she was kidding. "Hey, don't give me a bad time!" she whispered. "I wish I looked as awesome as you."

Hannah shook her head, but before she could answer, the signal came.

Remembering to walk slowly, Jill started down the aisle. When she reached the steps, she managed to get up them without tripping on her dress. Then she turned and looked toward the back of the church.

Next came Hannah and Morgan. Then Kelsey started forward. With her long white dress, she seemed to shimmer all the way down the aisle. *I've never seen her so beautiful!* thought Jill.

Kelsey's face shone. When she and Adam turned toward the altar, he looked just as happy and excited.

No one will ever love me like that, Jill thought.

During the pastor's message Jill wondered if everyone was looking at her. She did all she could not to fidget. But soon Kelsey and Adam exchanged rings, and it was time for Jill to walk back up the aisle.

At the wedding reception, Gran found her. "Jill, your hair is lovely that way!"

"Oh, Gran, I just couldn't get it the way I wanted!"

"You couldn't possibly improve on how it is," answered Gran. "And your dress brings out the color in your eyes."

Jill sighed. "I don't like the way it looks on me. Hannah looks so much nicer than I do."

Gran's smile faded. Her voice was gentle, yet firm. "Jill, I gave you two compliments."

Gran moved away, and Jill felt uneasy. *What was she telling me?*

As Jill watched, Gran walked over to Hannah and her boyfriend, Steve. Looking at Hannah, then at Gran, Steve grinned. Jill heard the low rumble of his voice.

"How about this really special girl? I found a really good one, don't you think, Gran?"

Hannah blushed but smiled up at him. "Thanks, Steve. I'm glad you like the way I am."

Steve's slow smile reached his eyes. In that moment something clicked in Jill's mind. *So that's what Gran meant!*

As Hannah and Steve turned toward Jill, Steve let out a low whistle. "Whew! You're all grown-up, Jill! I thought you were your sister Morgan coming over here!"

Out of long habit Jill almost answered, "Oh no, I don't look as nice as Morgan."

But in that instant she remembered Gran, and Jill found some words to match her grown-up look. "Thanks, Steve. I'm glad you like the way I look."

When Hannah and Gran smiled, Jill knew she'd given the right answer.

TO TALK ABOUT

▸ What is a compliment?

▸ When Hannah and Gran complimented Jill, what did she do? How do you suppose Jill's answers made Gran and Hannah feel? Why did it sound as if Jill wanted more compliments?

▸ If you respond to a compliment in the right way, you not only say thank you. You also make the other person feel good about giving the compliment. What did Hannah say that made Steve feel that way?

▸ Can you think of a time when someone complimented you? What did that person say? How did it make you feel? What would be a good way to answer that compliment?

▸ When we give a compliment, it's important to pick out something we honestly like. Otherwise, what we say doesn't ring true and sounds phony. Is there someone you'd like to encourage by giving a compliment? What can you say?

If you continually put yourself down, it's the same as saying you don't like the way God made you. How do you think Jesus sees you? What has He done that helps you know how much He cares about you?

▸ **In the Bible God the Father gave Jesus the ultimate compliment. Speaking from a cloud, God said, "This is my Son, whom I love; with him I am well pleased. Listen to him!"** (Matthew 17:5). Awesome, huh?

Kind words are like honey—sweet to the taste and good for your health. Proverbs 16:24 (TEV)

Thank you, Jesus, that compliments are special gifts. Thanks for the good way they make me feel. Help me know what to say when people compliment me. And help me encourage others with honest compliments.

Little Brother

Tyler stood at the door of his bedroom. He felt like a Fourth of July firecracker with a short fuse. Another second and his temper would explode.

It's bad enough sharing a room with Jesse, Tyler thought. *Now he's playing with my models!*

Only last night Tyler had finished a new rocket. Carefully he set it on top of the dresser, far back so no one would knock it off. But now Jesse had it on the floor, playing with it.

"Jes-s-s-see!" warned Tyler.

Looking up, his little brother tried to hide the model behind his back. Instead, his hand slipped and came down hard. The fins of the rocket broke off.

As Tyler started across the room, his anger exploded. Jesse took one look at his big brother and yelled, "Mom-m-m-m-my!"

Halfway to Jesse, Tyler stopped, but his anger didn't go away. He'd worked hard on that model. He had big dreams for how it would go into orbit.

"You can yell all you want," he told Jesse. "Mom's not here. I'm in charge, and you're gonna mind me!"

Jesse's eyes filled with tears. Scooting away from Tyler,

he slid under the bunk bed and crawled as far back in as he could.

Tyler crouched down. He had never been so angry in his life! "How come you keep taking my models? You're not supposed to touch them!"

In his hiding place under the bed, Jesse sniffed.

"What's the matter with you?" Tyler demanded.

Jesse's long, deep breath ended in a sob.

Tyler reached under the bed. Grabbing Jesse's arm, he started pulling him out. But just then he caught sight of his little brother's eyes. They were filled with panic.

Tyler felt ashamed. *Sure, Jesse did something wrong. He took my prize model, but what about me? I'm mad enough to really hurt him!*

Tyler dropped his brother's arm, backed off, and sat down on the floor. "Okay, Jesse, come on out."

Jesse didn't move.

"Come on out, I said."

Slowly and quietly Jesse moved out, then huddled in the corner of the room farthest from Tyler.

"What do you say, Jesse?"

Again Jesse drew a sobbing breath. "I'm sorry," he mumbled at last.

Tyler could hardly hear him. "Okay, I forgive you. But it's not gonna happen again, do you hear?"

Slowly Jesse nodded, his small lips puckered, the tears spilling out of his eyes onto his cheeks.

"If you forget, I'm gonna—" Tyler tightened his fists.

Suddenly he stopped, ashamed again. As he opened his fists, he remembered. *Is this the little brother I wanted?* Long ago, Tyler had prayed for a brother.

Again he felt ashamed. Ashamed of how angry he felt.

Ashamed that he had frightened Jesse. Sitting there on the floor, Tyler offered a quick, silent prayer. *Help me, God. Jesse shouldn't have taken the rocket, but what about me? What should I do?*

For a moment longer Tyler sat there. "Hmm. Why didn't I think of that before?"

Then he jumped up. "Come on, Jesse, I need some help."

His little brother came out of the corner slowly. Together they went to the basement and found the old painted boards Tyler remembered seeing. "Somewhere there are bricks," he told Jesse.

When they discovered those in the garage, Tyler carried everything to the bedroom. Before long he had put together a bookshelf.

"Okay," he said to Jesse. "From now on, this one's yours." He patted the shelf closest to the floor.

"And this one's mine." Tyler pointed to the top shelf. "I'll put my models here. You can see them, but you don't touch one thing on this shelf. Okay?"

The little boy nodded.

"Promise?" asked Tyler, still wondering if Jesse would remember.

"Promise," Jesse said.

"Tell you what," said Tyler. "If you don't touch my rockets, I'll take you to the field when I launch them. Not every time. But the first time I send one up. Okay?"

"Promise?" asked Jesse, his eyes lighting up.

"Promise," Tyler said.

Looking at his little brother, Tyler decided he wasn't such a bad little kid after all.

TO **TALK** ABOUT

▸ Why is it important that Jesse learn to not touch Tyler's things?

▸ Why is it necessary that Tyler learn to control his temper?

▸ What choices did Tyler make in working out his problem?

▸ Do you think his solution will work? Why or why not?

▸ Do you have a little brother or sister who makes you upset? What are some of the problems you face? In what practical ways can you solve those problems?

▸ What can Tyler do if he has a problem with Jesse that he can't solve? Whom could Tyler talk to? What are some things he could say?

▸ **Jesus taught that we reap what we sow. That means that what we give comes back to us.** If you are kind to others, that will come back to you. It may not happen in the next moment or even the next month, but eventually it will, often in a way you don't expect. Try to think of ways that has happened to you.

It is better to be slow-tempered than famous; it is better to have self-control than to control an army. Proverbs 16:32 (TLB)

Forgive me, Jesus, when I let my temper get out of control. Help me talk with the right person about the things that make me angry. Help us to figure out ways to make things better.

Erin's High Dive

Step by step, Erin climbed the ladder to the high dive. When she reached the board, she looked down. At one side of the pool Tod and Lisa lay sunning themselves.

The three of them had come to the pool together, and Erin liked both Tod and Lisa. They always seemed more exciting than the kids she knew at church. But Erin often wondered how Tod and Lisa felt about her. *Do they really like me? I don't feel like I fit in.*

Then Erin thought about her dive. She never grew tired of those seconds between leaving the board and breaking the water. Most of the time she felt excited, but also scared.

"When you get started, keep going," Mom told her once. "Don't change your mind in the middle of the air."

Whenever Mom and Dad could, they cheered Erin on. Just thinking about them helped her sometimes.

Now Erin took three quick steps and a jump, and pushed off the end of the board. Springing into the air, she spread her arms wide in a swan dive. Her body made the arc, swung down. An instant later she brought her arms above her head and sliced the water like a knife.

As Erin rose to the surface, she felt excited. *That was a good one!* she thought. Wiping the water out of her eyes, she looked around. Tod and Lisa were sitting up. *They're so busy talking. Did they see my dive?*

Erin's strokes slowed, then stopped, as she reached the edge of the pool. Pulling herself from the water, she tried to shrug aside her left-out feeling. As she lay down on her towel, she looked like one of them. But inside she felt set apart from Lisa and Tod. She wanted to belong.

Tod looked her way. "Ready to go?"

"We've only been here half an hour," Erin blurted out. "What's the big rush?"

But Tod's dark eyes looked bored. He was ready to move on, and Erin knew Lisa would go with him. She'd do whatever Tod did.

Is this like another high dive? Erin wanted to go with them, but she felt uncomfortable. Trying to push aside her uneasiness, she picked up her towel and sunglasses and stood up.

As they left the pool, Tod led the way. Soon he swung onto a path leading to the trees on the far side of the park. His lazy smile creased his face. "Good dive you made."

Erin warmed to his praise. "Oh, thanks!" But a moment later her wondering returned. "Where're we going?" she asked.

Without answering, Tod kept moving, and Lisa stayed at his side. Suddenly Erin guessed why they were heading for the trees. Was it their new meeting place? Her steps slowed.

Tod turned. "Come on. What's taking you so long?"

Looking at him, Erin thought again how much she liked Tod, how much she'd like to fit in with his friends. Yet she also felt as if a mysterious hand pushed her toward something that made her afraid.

What will it be this time? she wondered. *Booze? Pot? Hard drugs?*

As they neared the trees, Erin smelled the scent of pot. She stopped on the path. "I don't want anything to do with marijuana," she said.

"It won't hurt you any."

"That's not true," Erin told him. "It can hurt both my body and my mind. I don't want to get dependent on any drug."

Tod smirked. "You're crazy! Dumb, dumb, dumb!"

Erin hated his laugh. It had a hard sound to it and always made her feel left out. *Maybe I should give it a try,* she thought. *Maybe I would finally fit in.*

"Everybody does it," Tod said as though he had heard her thoughts. Lisa looked as if she agreed.

I know grass is bad for me, Erin thought with one part of her mind. *I know it could start a habit.* But the other part of her mind tried to push those thoughts aside. *Nothing could happen to me.*

Then she remembered Mom's words about diving: *"Don't change your mind in the middle of the air."*

Erin drew a deep breath. "I don't wanna try it," she said again. "I'm going back to the pool."

"What are you, a wimp or something?" When Tod spoke, his words had a cruel edge. "Or do you think you're better than we are?"

Knifelike, the words cut, but Erin looked Tod in the eye. "I said no, and I mean no. Don't ever ask me again."

Turning, she started back to the pool—half running, half walking so Tod wouldn't see the tears in her eyes.

Then she heard a voice behind her. "Hey, just a minute," Lisa called. "I'm coming with you."

As Lisa caught up, Erin slowed her steps and blinked away the tears. Relieved now, she also felt surprised. *What if I hadn't said no? Right now Lisa would be saying yes.*

TO **TALK** ABOUT

▶ Why do you suppose Tod and Lisa seemed more exciting to Erin than the kids at church? Why do you think kids get involved with drugs?

▶ What was Tod offering Erin—friendship or the pressure to do something that would hurt her? What do you think is a smart way to handle pressure from the kids you know?

▶ **Someone who is really a friend won't ask you to do something that will hurt you.** Do you feel Tod was a true friend? Describe the qualities you want your friends to have.

▶ Is it worth having a friend like Tod? Why or why not?

▶ If you desperately want to be popular, how can it affect the choices you make?

▶ Erin wanted to fit in with Tod and his friends, but she felt uneasy. **A feeling of uneasiness can be the Holy Spirit's warning.** Why is it good if you feel uncomfortable with some kids? How can that feeling protect you?

▶ Do you think Erin stuck to her decision to say no? Why or why not? What does it mean to stand firm in a choice? In what ways can you say no so that kids know you really mean it?

▶ If you don't have a dad or mom who supports you in making right choices, where can you find friends and adults who will help you?

‣ **Courage is going beyond your fear of what others think in order to do the right thing.** If you have memorized Bible verses, those words can come to you at the moment you need them. If you repeat those words when you're tempted to do something wrong, you'll have a laser sword against the enemy. Check out these verses about courage: Joshua 1:9; 2 Kings 6:16; Isaiah 41:13; 43:1–3a; Hebrews 13:5–6.

‣ See how many more courage verses you can find. Copy them down in one place or write them on 3 × 5 index cards you can look at often. How about picking out a verse right now and memorizing it?

"The Lord is my light and my salvation—whom shall I fear? The Lord is the stronghold of my life—of whom shall I be afraid?" (Psalm 27:1).

"Be strong and courageous. Do not be afraid or terrified because of them, for the Lord your God goes with you; he will never leave you nor forsake you." Deuteronomy 31:6

Thank you, Jesus, that I don't feel comfortable with some kids. Thanks for protecting me that way. Whenever I face something that would hurt me, give me the strength to say no and stick to it.

Tree House for Michael

For Michael the July afternoon seemed to last forever. *If I still lived in Annandale, I'd have plenty to do*, he thought. Two weeks before, he and Mom and Dad had moved to a new town. So far Michael hadn't made any friends.

Before moving, he knew lots of kids, and most of them he liked. It didn't seem to matter that he had no brothers or sisters. Now the house seemed awfully quiet when he was home alone. He'd been trying to fill up the empty spaces by surfing the Net, but he wished he had a friend he could see.

Then when Michael went into the garage, he made a discovery. The people who lived there before had left all kinds of things. As soon as Dad drove into the garage, Michael pounced on him. "Can I have the two-by-fours and those old storm windows and the boards leaning against the wall?"

Dad held up his hands. "Hey, slow down! Why do you need them?"

"I've always wanted a tree house. We've never had a place for one before."

"Hmm," said Dad, not seeming surprised. Michael was always thinking up projects. "Where do you want it?"

Michael led the way around the house. Their backyard opened onto a large marsh. A tall oak stood on a rise overlooking the cattails that lined the shore.

"See those two branches?" Walking around the trunk, Michael pointed upward. "The door could be right there, and the ladder on this side."

"Hmm," Dad said again.

"Three windows—one on each side and the fourth side for the door."

"Wel-l-l-l." Dad walked around the tree, checking it from every angle. "Yup. It would work. But I'd like to help a bit so we can make it safe."

"All riiiight!" exclaimed Michael.

And so the work began. Dad and Michael went to the lumberyard and bought extra-long two-by-sixes. That night they nailed one of them across two branches and over to the trunk. They used the other as an extra brace that stretched to a nearby maple.

Early the next morning Michael and his dad started building again. During the next week they worked whenever Dad had spare time. First came the base for the floor. Then the walls went up and the roof. Together they worked until the tree house was finished.

Finally Dad climbed down the ladder. "Well, Michael, it's all yours!"

"Hey, that's right," said Michael, feeling proud of what they had built. "It's all mine!"

As they put their tools in the garage, a boy rode his bike down the street. When he looked through the side yard to the tree house, he skidded to a stop.

"I'm Derek," he said to Michael as he dropped his bike on the ground. "I live a couple blocks from here."

As soon as Michael introduced himself, Derek exclaimed, "What a great tree house you've got! Can I see it, Mike?"

"Uh, sure," Michael said. It seemed strange to be called Mike again. Only his friends in Annandale called him that. Leading Derek into the backyard, he started up the ladder.

Rung by rung, Derek followed him. "Wow!" he said as he peered through the window overlooking the marsh. "What a great clubhouse this would be!"

"A clubhouse?" A secret hope filled Michael. Joining Derek at the window, he looked down through the leaves. "What do you mean?"

"Me and Seth and Josiah have a science club. We've been looking for a place to meet. We could bring binoculars and watch the birds and beavers in the marsh."

Michael liked the idea. *A science club could be really fun! Then I'd have some friends!* But he was afraid to let himself hope.

Then he had an awful thought. *What if they wreck my tree house?* Once he'd let a kid borrow his bike. When the kid totaled it, he never paid Michael back.

Feeling torn inside, Michael wondered what to say. He was still wondering when he started back down the ladder. *I want new friends, but I'm scared. What should I do?*

As Michael reached the ground, he figured it out. *I'll show 'em how to take care of it*, he decided. *We'll have some club rules.*

When Derek swung onto his bike, he grinned. "So long, Mike. I'll bring back the guys. Okay?"

"Okay!" Mike exclaimed. Inside, he felt okay, too.

TO **TALK** ABOUT

▸ If Mike chooses to share the tree house, what do you think will happen to his loneliness? How can sharing be a way of making friends?

▸ When you share, it doesn't mean you let kids do whatever they want with your things. They should respect your rights. Do you think Mike's new friends will be careful with the tree house? What can he do if they aren't?

▸ Have you ever been afraid to share and it turned out all right? Tell about it. What did you learn?

▸ Like Michael, all of us need friends. We also need to know that God can help us if we're lonely. In what ways has God helped you in a lonely time?

▸ **If Jesus is your forever Friend, He can help you with your other friendships.** Talk about ways Jesus wants to help you every day.

[Jesus said], "Give to others, and God will give to you. In-deed, you will receive a full measure, a generous helping, poured into your hands—all that you can hold. The measure you use for others is the one that God will use for you." Luke 6:38 (TEV)

When I'm lonely, Lord, remind me that you're with me. Show me how to share and how to make new friends. Thanks for being my very best Friend.

Kari's Burnt Offering

When the phone call came that morning, Kari didn't know what to do.

"Sorry for asking so late," said the woman at the other end of the line. "We have so many people who want to come to our program tonight that we need one more cake. Would your mom possibly have time to make it?"

Kari thought for a moment. Sandy was one of Mom's best friends. She wouldn't ask a favor unless she really needed help. And besides, the program that evening was sponsored by their home educators' group. Kari loved to get together with the other students who were being homeschooled by their parents.

"Mom isn't here right now," Kari answered. "Grandma fell, and Mom went to help her. She probably won't get home until late this afternoon. But I can make the cake."

"Oh, would you, Kari?" Relief filled Sandy's voice. "It would help me so much!"

"No problem," Kari answered. "I'll be glad to do it."

But when she got off the phone, Kari felt a moment of panic. She knew exactly what she'd like to bake—the German chocolate cake their family often enjoyed. But did Mom have the ingredients on hand? Her shopping day was tomorrow, and Kari had no way of getting to the store. To make matters worse, Dad wouldn't be home from work until just before the meeting.

In the cupboard Kari found Mom's recipes, then the one she needed. Next Kari checked for ingredients. One white cake mix. One package instant pudding mix. Two eggs. Two cups milk. Then brown sugar, margarine, milk, coconut, and walnuts for the frosting.

One by one, Kari set the ingredients on the counter. She had only one cake mix and one chocolate pudding mix, but that was all she needed.

Kari sighed with relief. *That was a close call!*

In no time at all, she had the ingredients blended together, poured into the pan, and in the oven. With the timer set, she took out a kettle and started the frosting. As she melted the margarine and added the brown sugar, she felt good about what she was doing. Already Sandy appreciated her help, and Mom would feel the same way when she got home.

German chocolate cake was Kari's favorite. Even now she imagined her friends gathering around, telling her how great her cake looked and tasted. *I want it to be just perfect!*

But when the timer dinged and Kari opened the oven to take out the cake, she gasped. "Oh no!"

On one end, the cake was high, nearly reaching the top of the pan. On the other end the cake was low, less than an inch high. At one spot in the middle, the cake rose in a slight mound. Otherwise it was all at a slant.

Kari groaned. *There's my perfect cake, all right. How did I manage to do that?*

Carefully she set the cake to cool, then opened the oven again. Before her eyes was the rack on which the cake had baked. Only now did Kari remember wiping it off three nights before and putting it back in the oven. She groaned. *I didn't push it in right!* she realized. On one side the rack was higher than on the other.

More than that, she should have put the rack in the middle of the oven, instead of its lowest position.

"What on earth will I do?" Kari asked herself, so upset that she spoke out loud.

Frantically she looked through the cupboards again, hoping that somehow there was a cake mix she had missed. Partway through Kari's search, the frosting boiled up and over. Grabbing the kettle, she turned down the heat and went back to her search.

Not one more cake mix. Not one more pudding mix.

Swallowing hard, she blinked away tears. *So. I can't make another cake.*

When the frosting finished boiling, Kari knew she had to use it. It was supposed to go on while the cake was still warm. *Maybe I can heap it up at the low end.*

Starting at the high end of the cake, she spooned out the frosting. Like a sled running downhill, the brown sugar syrup found a path. Kari sighed.

When she finished frosting the cake, she had done all she could to make the low end look high. But there was still close to an inch difference between the two ends of the cake.

I can keep it at home and pretend I forgot to bring it, Kari told herself. *Or I can sneak it into the kitchen at church. I'll cover it with tinfoil and not put my name on the pan. I'll set it on that counter next to the back door. Maybe no one will see it there. Maybe they won't need to use it.*

But that night when Kari and her family reached the

church where the homeschoolers met, none of those things worked.

Mom's friend Sandy met Kari at the door of the kitchen. "Oh, Kari, you saved my life!" she exclaimed. "What would I do without you?"

"My cake is really awful—" Kari started to say. But she didn't even get the words out.

"Just set it on the table with the other cakes," Sandy told her. "I'll cut it in a minute. We're almost ready to eat."

Kari gulped. As her friends gathered around, she almost panicked. *I have never been so embarrassed in my whole life! They'll think I can't bake a simple cake!*

She was right. When Kari took off the cover, Sandy's son, Isaac, looked over her shoulder.

"That's a goofy-looking cake," he said. But then he pointed. "If I take from that end, I'll get the biggest piece!"

Already Sandy was back with a knife and spatula. Before she began cutting, Kari decided what to do. *I can put myself down and feel bruised all over. Or I can make a joke of it.*

"Just a minute," Kari told Sandy. "Before you begin cutting, I need to explain how to make this cake."

Kari's friends gathered around, some standing across the table and others looking over her shoulder. Kari pointed to the high end of the cake. "You set the oven rack at an angle," she began.

Looking up, she caught a hint of laughter in the eyes of her friend Elise. "Then you bake the cake without opening the door to look at it." The girl next to Elise grinned.

"After it's well set so you can't change anything, you open the oven door and look in."

A second girl giggled. Sandy's lips twitched, and a sparkle lit her eyes.

"Let the frosting boil over," Kari went on. "Then heap what's left at the top of the hill and let it slide down."

When Isaac and Elise started laughing, Kari's other friends joined in. But Kari felt warmed by their laughter. *They're laughing with me, not at me*, she thought, and she, too, began to laugh.

"It's going to be the best cake I've ever eaten," Sandy said. "You help serve it, okay?"

As people came through the line, they had their choice of cakes, but every one of Kari's close friends took a piece from her. "I have to try this," said more than one.

The cake was half gone when Kari made another discovery. Under the raised place in the middle lay a dark brown circle of burnt cake.

Kari gulped and remembered the oven rack set too close to the gas flame. But quick as a wink she had another idea. Pushing in the spatula, she cut the piece off halfway up, leaving the burnt part in the pan. For each person receiving a piece, Kari offered her biggest smile.

As she finished dishing up her hilly burnt offering, Sandy brought out still another cake. That one, of course, looked absolutely perfect. For a moment Kari had one twinge of regret, one wish that she could have done better. Then she pushed the thought aside.

I did the best I could, she told herself. *That's more important than being perfect.*

Kari's friends seemed to think so, too.

TO **TALK** ABOUT

▸ No matter who you are, you might someday bake a lopsided cake. That's because every one of us makes mistakes. You can look at a mistake, fold up with embarrassment, and put yourself down. Or you can decide what attitude you want to take. What choice did Kari make in how she looked at her mistakes?

▸ Have you had times when you tried to do something well and it didn't work? Describe something in which you really goofed up. How did you feel about what happened? What did you do about your mistakes?

▸ Most of us take ourselves too seriously. If you make a mistake, will it be the end of the world? How do you know? What's the difference between putting yourself down and making a healthy joke? Which was Kari doing?

▸ **Feeling you have to be perfect can keep you from trying at all.** In what ways do you want to do your best but also know that it's okay to not be perfect? Clue: It might help to think about winning in sports, giving a speech, playing a keyboard, or singing a solo.

▸ **How you feel about yourself comes back to you.** If you keep telling yourself that you aren't worth anything, you reflect that attitude to others. You invite people to treat you as though you're not worth anything. Instead, **if you *know* that Jesus cares about you as one very special kid, you can reflect that.** In what ways do you know that God values you as a person?

▸ If you know that you are loved and valued by the people who are important to you, it helps you to be more loving. But feelings go up and down. None of us can always feel we are loved. People who are happy have learned a big secret—to forget about themselves and reach out to help others. Who are some famous people who have done that?

What are some practical things you can do and say to encourage the people around you?

Remember this: Whoever sows sparingly will also reap sparingly, and whoever sows generously will reap generously.
2 Corinthians 9:6

Lord Jesus, I want to do the best I can with the gifts and abilities you have given me. But I also want the ability to laugh at myself and get up and go on. Help me to sow good things—give good things into the lives of others. Because you're my forever Friend, I know you'll help me do that. Thanks!

Late for Supper

"Bye, Alex. See you tomorrow," called Colin.

The door closed behind him. A moment later it popped open again.

"Hey, Colin, wait a minute. I forgot to show you my new video game."

Colin turned and leapfrogged back up the steps. He liked Alex's new game. Yet he felt uneasy and kept glancing at his watch.

Finally Colin pulled away. "I really have to go. I promised Mom I'd be home at four-thirty, and it's already five."

This time Colin half walked, half ran down the sidewalk. The early January twilight shut him into a gray-blue world. Ahead of him the streetlight turned on. Soon it would be dark.

I'll head down Main Street, he thought. It was a block longer going that way, but there would be more lights and people.

Passing the gas station and post office, Colin started to jog. Just then he heard a shout. "Hey, wait for me!"

A moment later, Neal caught up to him. "Come here, Colin. I want you to see something."

Colin shook his head. "I'm already late. I promised Mom—"

"It'll just take a minute. Smitty's got in some new telescopes. Come on. You'll like them."

Colin hesitated.

"Just one quick look," Neal said. "No one will notice if you're late."

Colin thought a moment. *Maybe he's right. Mom is probably working, and Dad usually gets home late. What difference will it make that I said four-thirty?*

"Okay, but only for a minute," he answered.

Half an hour later, Colin left the store and once more headed for home. Now it was truly dark. The blackness of night hung around him, and cold stung his cheeks. His uneasiness grew.

Two more blocks, he thought, starting to jog again. Then to his relief a car pulled up alongside him. In the darkness the man inside looked like Colin's neighbor.

Colin felt relieved. *I'll get a ride home and be there faster*. Besides, it would feel good to get in out of the cold. But when the man spoke, Colin realized he was a stranger.

"I've lost my dog," the man said.

"Oh, I'm sorry!" Colin had lost his own dog once and knew how awful it felt. "What does your dog look like?"

"He's a little wiener dog named Oscar Meyer." The man motioned Colin to come closer. "Here. I'll show you a photo."

Colin started forward, then remembered Dad's long-ago warning.

"Will you help me find him?" the man asked, holding out the photo.

Instead, Colin stepped back, out of reach, and spoke quickly. "I'll run home and tell my mom you lost your dog.

She'll know the best way to help you."

Breaking into a jog again, he headed down the sidewalk as fast as he could go. When he turned the corner into his own street, he looked toward home. The outside light and every light in the house was on. *Uh-oh!* Colin thought.

Now, instead of hurrying, his feet dragged. As Colin started up the walk, he wished he didn't have to go inside. At the same time he felt afraid not to. Through the window he saw Mom on the phone. Behind her, seeming to wait for the answer, stood Dad.

I'll tell them that Alex held me up. Then it was Neal's fault. Slowly Colin opened the door.

TO TALK ABOUT

▸ What does it mean to make a promise? When we make a promise, why is it important that we don't break it?

▸ Why do you think Colin's mother was phoning someone?

▸ Whose fault was it that Colin was late? When did Colin make his most important choice about what time he was going to get home?

▸ If his parents weren't there, would it make any difference whether Colin got home at four-thirty? Why or why not?

▸ If Colin had a habit of always being late, his parents would never know when to expect him. What would happen if Colin had trouble on the way home and no one knew there was something wrong? Explain.

▸ When a stranger stopped to talk, Colin did two important things: 1) He stayed back from the car, out of the man's reach. 2) Instead of following a man he didn't know, Colin

----

chose to leave. Why are both of those decisions important?

▶ Can you think of a time when you obeyed your parents, even though it was hard, and it turned out well? Describe what happened.

▶ **Why does your forever Friend Jesus want to be with you all the time?** How can He help you live in the commandment about your parents?

Children, obey your parents in the Lord, for this is right. "Honor your father and mother"—which is the first commandment with a promise—"that it may go well with you and that you may enjoy long life on the earth." Ephesians 6:1-3

Jesus, so often I want to do what I want to do. Sometimes it gets in the way of what my parents want of me. Help me to honor them by thinking about their feelings and keeping my promises to them.

Friends at Any Price?

For as long as Jeremy could remember, Nolan had been his best friend at church. Jeremy liked it that way. It made him feel good to know that when the kids got together, he had someone special to do things with.

But now it looked as if that might change.

When the kids met at church to go bowling, a new boy showed up. For a few minutes he hung around the door, as though wondering if he should slip back out.

As Jeremy watched, Nolan went over to him. "I don't know your name," he said. "Are you new here?"

The boy nodded. "I'm André. We just moved here from Quebec."

Soon Nolan brought André over. "André, this is my friend Jeremy."

Jeremy grinned at André, but his heart wasn't in it. He didn't even try to make André feel at home.

Nolan didn't seem to notice. "My dad's driving us to the bowling alley," he told André. "You can ride with Jeremy and me."

When they reached the alley, the boys discovered that the girls had taken over most of the lanes. Jeremy had expected to bowl with Nolan. But there were only two places left on one lane and two on another.

As they waited in line for balls and shoes, Nolan whispered to Jeremy. "I'll bowl with André since he doesn't know anyone. Why don't you and Mark get together?"

Feeling lost and alone without his best friend, Jeremy found Mark. Jeremy didn't want to bowl with him. He didn't like the boys in their lane. He just wanted to keep Jeremy to himself. He wanted everything to be the way it used to be.

Two lanes over, Nolan and André started bowling. Watching them, Jeremy felt uneasy. *What if Jeremy likes André so much that he doesn't want to be my friend anymore?*

Trying to push the thought aside, Jeremy picked up his ball. His first try knocked down two pins. His next ball rolled into the gutter.

Jeremy pasted on a smile and hoped for better on his next turn. But his entire game was off. Whenever he sat down, he tried to watch two lanes over. He kept telling himself, *I wish I were there.*

When they started the next game, Mark tried to cheer up Jeremy. "Hey, come on, you can do better. You're a good bowler."

But just then Jeremy heard a shout. André had gotten a strike! Watching Nolan clap André on the back, Jeremy felt left out again.

In the second game he bowled even worse. A new thought haunted him. *What if I lose my best friend?*

On the way back to church, the boys were separated again. But when they got there, Jeremy slipped into the food line behind Nolan. "How did you bowl?" he asked.

"Great!" Nolan answered.

André turned around to listen, but Jeremy ignored him. "Did you do better than the other kids you were with?" Jeremy asked, still looking at Nolan.

"Nope," said Nolan. "But that's okay. It was the first time André bowled, and guess what? He got a strike!"

Jeremy didn't congratulate André on his strike. He didn't even look at the new boy. When André picked up his hamburger, Jeremy saw the unhappy look on his face. Half question, half hurt, his expression seemed to ask, "Is there something wrong with me?"

As Jeremy sat down at the table, he also saw Nolan's expression. *Uh-oh*, Jeremy thought. *I'm in trouble. Nolan doesn't like the way I'm acting. He knows I'm being mean to André.*

Suddenly a feeling of shame started way down in Jeremy's toes. In that moment he didn't like himself. But there was something that bothered Jeremy even more. *André is new here, and I've hurt him.*

Sitting there between Nolan and André, Jeremy asked himself one question: *What should I do?*

TO **TALK** ABOUT

▸ What do you think Jeremy did? Why?

▸ In what ways did Jeremy want to keep Nolan for himself?

▸ Why is it easy to ignore someone who's new? How did Jeremy do it to André?

▸ The Bible tells us that "love is not self-seeking." What does it mean to be self-seeking? How was Jeremy self-seeking? Why do you think this story is called "Friends at Any Price?"

▸ Has anyone ever treated you the way Jeremy treated

André? How did it feel to be ignored for a reason you didn't understand?

▸ Why did Jeremy treat André that way? What was Jeremy feeling inside? How have you felt when you thought you'd lose a good friend? What happened?

▸ Sometimes both grown-ups and kids are very possessive in the way they treat their friends. To have a good relationship it's important to give a friend enough space. What does it mean to give someone space? Why do good friends need to give each other the space to also be friends with other kids?

▸ What's the best way to keep a good friend? Try to give examples of what you mean.

▸ **Remember? Jesus promised to be your forever Friend.** In what ways can you use the Bible to get to know Jesus? What does it mean to have a *forever* Friend?

Help me, Jesus, when I get selfish and want to keep a friend all to myself. Help me give my friends the space they need to keep on being my friends.

[Love] is not rude, it is not self-seeking, it is not easily angered, it keeps no record of wrongs. 1 Corinthians 13:5

Oreo Goes to the Fair

At the county fair Cassidy led her calf inside a shed. As she tied Oreo's lead rope to a rail, she saw Paula heading her way. *Hope she doesn't come here,* Cassidy thought.

But Paula did. Bringing over her heifer,* a young cow that has never given birth, Paula took the space next to Oreo. As Cassidy said hi and tried to smile, she took a good look at Princess. Paula's entry in the fair competition could give Cassidy a good run for her money.

Feeling uneasy, she turned back to her own calf. Named Oreo because she was a black-and-white Holstein, the heifer acted as if she wasn't sure about her new surroundings. Cassidy kept talking to her. "It's okay, girl," she said, stroking her neck. "Settle down."

Born in January, Oreo would be one of the largest in her class. Cassidy felt proud of Oreo's shiny coat and the straight line of her back.

But Paula looked toward Oreo and said, "She's got a back like a camel."

Cassidy felt a hot flush go to her face. *How mean can you get?* she thought.

---

*pronounced hef-er

"A rea-a-al winner!" Paula drawled the words, and Cassidy knew she meant just the opposite.

Still Cassidy didn't answer. She and Paula were members of the same 4-H Club. Usually members worked together at fair time and helped each other. But Paula always picked on Cassidy. Last year their entries had been the same age and class. Now they were competing against each other again.

"Her eyes are too close together," Paula went on. "Looks like she has a brain the size of a peanut."

Cassidy's anger boiled up and spilled over. "What about Princess? She doesn't look so great!"

A half smile formed on Paula's lips, as if she was glad she had made Cassidy angry. Turning away, Paula got Princess a bucket of feed.

Cassidy washed down Oreo, then started to groom her. She'd taken care of the heifer since she was a newborn calf with wobbly legs and hair that was still wet. When Cassidy chose Oreo for her 4-H project, she began leading the calf around, teaching her to follow.

Cassidy's kindness to the young calf paid off. They became friends. Whenever Cassidy entered the pasture, Oreo came close and waited for Cassidy to scratch her neck and behind her ears.

Now Paula broke into Cassidy's thoughts. "Just because you won a blue ribbon last year doesn't mean you'll do it again."

"Is that what's bothering you? Because you got second place—a red ribbon?"

Paula tossed her head. "Of course not. The judge was playing favorites, and you know it."

Once more Cassidy's anger boiled up. As she brushed Oreo until her coat shone, she couldn't get Paula out of her mind. Cassidy didn't like being enemies with someone. Usually she found it easy to make friends. She'd even done it with a calf.

Just then an idea dropped into her mind. *Aha!* Cassidy bent down to hide her grin from Paula. *I'll be as nice to her as I am to Oreo.*

While clipping the hair around Oreo's ears, Cassidy decided what to do. She felt as if she'd be spitting through her teeth, but she'd give it a try.

When Paula finished brushing Princess, Cassidy turned to her. "Her coat looks nice and shiny."

Paula looked surprised but didn't say anything.

"You've done a good job of grooming her."

Still Paula looked surprised, as though she didn't trust Cassidy. But this time she mumbled thanks.

As Cassidy worked the end of Oreo's tail into many small braids, she felt different inside. She still didn't like being next to Paula, but at least she didn't feel as upset.

The next day Cassidy unbraided Oreo's tail and back-combed the kinky ends. As she fluffed them up, Cassidy looked over at Paula. "Your heifer looks great."

Again Paula looked as if she didn't know whether Cassidy was teasing. After a moment Paula seemed to decide Cassidy meant it. "So does yours," she said, her voice low.

When it was time for the judging, Cassidy changed into white clothes. If there was a tie between entries, even the appearance of the one showing an animal could make a difference in winning or losing. Then she attached a lead to Oreo's halter and fell into line. Paula and Princess followed them into the large, open space surrounded by bleachers.

As they walked in a circle, the judge called out, "Stop your heifers!" Then, "Pose them!"

Oreo stood with her front legs firmly beneath her. With the back leg closest to the judge forward, she kept the other leg straight.

Soon the judge began pulling animals out of the circle and placing them in lines—one line for the blue ribbons, another for the red, and so on. When the judge placed Oreo at the front of the blue ribbon line, Cassidy felt excited. *Maybe she'll get Grand Champion of our class!*

Paula's turn was next. The judge circled Princess, and Paula kept moving to the opposite side so she wouldn't block the judge's view. She looked sure of herself and Princess.

Cassidy caught her breath. For the first time she wondered, *Was Paula being mean so I'd feel jumpy and not do as well?*

A moment later the judge led Paula forward, putting her and Princess in front of Cassidy.

Outwardly Cassidy stood at attention, but inside she felt sick. *Paula's first, and I'm second. She'll get Grand Champion.*

Then Cassidy had an even worse thought. *Did I help Paula win by being nice to her? She looks so sure of herself.* In close competition Paula's attitude could make a difference.

As the judge circled the other calves, the awful question stayed with Cassidy. Watching the judge, Cassidy kept Oreo alert. But Paula glanced toward the stands and smiled.

In that moment the judge glanced her way. *He must have seen Paula*, Cassidy thought. *She shouldn't have looked at the stands. She looks too sure of herself.*

The judge returned to their line and asked Cassidy more questions. When he told her to move in front of Paula, Cassidy hardly dared breathe.

A moment later the judge brought out the Grand Champion ribbon. "I place Oreo at the top of the class," he called out. "She's an outstanding heifer and responds well to her owner."

Then the judge handed the ribbon and trophy to Cassidy. *Grand Champion? Best in show?* Cassidy felt like crying and laughing at the same time.

The judge moved on and gave Paula a blue ribbon. Watching her, Cassidy wondered, *How's she gonna feel— missing it by one wrong move?*

Soon the 4-H'ers began leading their heifers back to the shed. Cassidy felt like shouting, but Paula was quiet the whole way. When they finally stopped their calves at a rail, Paula looked at Cassidy. "Congratulations," Paula told her. "You deserved it."

"Thanks!" Cassidy felt relieved that the competition between them was gone. "But you were just a hair's breath away. It was really close."

Then Cassidy flung her arms around Oreo. When she looked up, she saw Paula's grin. *I've won more than a trophy*, Cassidy decided.

TO **TALK** ABOUT

▸ What did Cassidy mean by thinking, *I've won more than a trophy?*

▸ Why can it be especially hard to be nice to someone you compete against?

▸ Cassidy learned something from Oreo that helped her decide how to act toward Paula. What was it?

▸ How does putting down another person destroy a friendship? Why does encouragement help a friendship grow? Why can encouragement be called a put-up instead of a put-down?

▸ Do you have a pet you love very much? If so, why does that animal mean a lot to you?

▸ How does your pet encourage you? How has your pet helped you know how to treat people?

▸ When you compete against others, there can be hard lessons to learn. At the end of a game, players go down a line, shaking hands with players on the other team. Why do they do this? What do you think they're saying?

▸ **Did Jesus give people put-ups or put-downs?** Give reasons for your answer, then check out Matthew 22:34–39.

into friends.

Thank you, God, for creating all kinds of animals for us to enjoy. Thanks for how much my special pet means to me. When kids upset me, help me act in a way that pleases you. Thanks that you can turn even my enemies

friends. Proverbs 16:7 (TEV)

When you please the Lord, you can make your enemies into

Someone in the Kitchen

"See you, Joey!" Nicholas waved good-bye and started up the driveway. He was whistling when he reached the house.

But when he got to the door, Nicholas stopped. As though putting on a mask, he let his face go blank. Not for anything would he let his stepmother know that things had gone better at school.

The night before, Marcy and Dad had prayed for him. *I won't tell her about it*, Nicholas decided. *She'll think it's because they prayed.*

For the millionth time Nicholas thought about Mom. She had died two years ago, but sometimes he still ached inside. *It was bad enough for her to die. Why did Dad have to get married again?*

Marcy was in the kitchen when Nicholas walked in. "How did it go today?" she asked.

Usually Nicholas pretended he didn't hear her, but this time he couldn't. "Oh, I don't know," he said, and kept moving.

As he entered the family room, he stopped in his tracks. "You changed it!"

"I worked on it all day," said Marcy. "How do you like it?"

"I don't." Nicholas kicked at the sofa. "I can't stand it.

Why did you have to make it different?"

Marcy blinked. Something deep in her eyes looked hurt. Then the moment passed. "It's important that the house feels comfortable to me—that it reflects who I am—that it reflects my tastes."

Nicholas broke in. "I don't like your tastes. I like the way Mom left it."

Again Nicholas saw the shadow deep in Marcy's eyes. She walked over to a window. For a moment she stood there, looking out. When she turned back, the hurt look was gone.

"Nick, I'm not trying to take your mother's place. She was a lovely woman. But none of us can change the fact that she died."

This time Nicholas turned away. He didn't want to listen, but Marcy kept on.

"Your dad and I were both lonely. He felt he needed my help, and we love each other."

Marcy's voice sounded strange. In spite of himself, Nicholas looked at her.

"I'm not perfect," she said. "But I'm trying my best. You can choose to like me or not like me. If you decide you don't want to like me, there's nothing I can do about it."

Nicholas squirmed. He knew that what Marcy was saying was true, but he didn't want to think about it. It made him too uncomfortable. At the same time, he had to admit that Marcy had guts.

As soon as he could, Nicholas escaped to his room. When he came to supper, he picked at his meal. If Marcy tried to talk with him, he looked at his plate and mumbled. But when Dad spoke, Nicholas acted interested and answered his questions.

In the days that followed, Nicholas often felt torn apart

inside. Sometimes he felt lonesome for Mom. If only she could come back, they'd have good talks again.

Mom had been sick for a long time. Sometimes Nicholas wondered if it was his fault that she died. Whenever he thought about that, he took it out on Marcy. He picked apart everything she did, even the cookies she baked.

"Why didn't you make chocolate chip instead of peanut butter?" he asked her one day. "I don't like peanut butter." Yet when she wasn't around, he sneaked the cookies out of the kitchen.

Sometimes he heard Dad and Marcy laugh together. Nicholas knew that when he was with them, they never did. *Good*, he thought. *I'm making Marcy feel bad.*

Then one day everything changed. When Nicholas came home from school, Marcy wasn't there. The house was empty. A note on the table said that she needed to fly home.

At supper Dad explained. "Her mother is very sick. Marcy is the only one who can help."

It wasn't long before Nicholas got tired of eating TV dinners again. He'd forgotten what it was like to wash his own clothes. But most of all, he missed having someone in the kitchen when he came home. He missed *her*.

Finally one day Nicholas asked, "When is Marcy coming back?"

"I don't know," Dad answered. "She's trying to find an opening for her mother in a nursing home. Her mom is too sick to fly here."

As the weeks stretched into a month, Nicholas noticed the empty house even more. One afternoon he thought about how he felt whenever he was mean to Marcy. *When I try to hate her, I find all kinds of things wrong with her.*

A strange new thought came to him. *"You can choose to like me,"* Marcy had said.

That night Nicholas made a choice. Long ago Mom had told him how to pray. And so he asked, "Jesus, please forgive me. Forgive me for all the mean things I've said to Marcy."

A few days passed, and the struggle Nicholas had felt faded into the background. But he still found himself thinking about Marcy's words. Then one week later she was in the kitchen when Nicholas came home.

When he saw her, Nicholas remembered his prayer. Suddenly he felt scared. "Oh wow! What do I do now?"

TO **TALK** ABOUT

▸ When we don't talk about the things that bother us, we become like a shaken-up can of soda. The moment we open it, the soda fizzes out in all directions. Who would be a good person for Nicholas to talk with? How could he begin?

▸ What if Nicholas said, "I feel guilty about . . ." and finished the sentence? What do you think his dad would say?

▸ After someone dies people often feel guilty about something that couldn't be helped. How do you know it wasn't Nick's fault that his mother died?

▸ How did his guilty feelings hurt his relationship with Marcy?

▸ If you choose to *not* like someone, what kinds of things do you notice about that person? If you choose to *like* someone, what kinds of things do you notice?

▸ Is there someone you often need to be with, even though

you don't like that person? What choice can you make? How do you think it will affect the way you feel about each other?

▸ When Jesus was with His disciples, they didn't always act the way He wanted. Because they expected Him to become an earthly king, they even argued about who would be the greatest. Jesus also knew that one of His disciples, Judas, would betray Him. Yet Jesus was not rude to him. What does being rude mean? What is a more grown-up way to behave?

▸ How can Jesus help you choose to like a new stepparent, stepbrother, or stepsister? How can Jesus help you in your relationships with your birth family (the family into which you were born)?

▸ **In what ways can Jesus be your forever Friend, no matter what happens to you?**

We love because God first loved us. 1 John 4:19 (TEV)

When I feel mixed-up inside, I take it out on people around me. Forgive me, Jesus. Help me sort out my feelings. In your big, strong name, Jesus, I choose to like the people I need to get along with. Help me to see and appreciate good things about them. Thank you!

The Big Choice

"Krista-a-a-a-a!" came a little voice from the bedroom.

"Just a minute," said Krista into the phone. She was baby-sitting at the Perrys' again. Cupping her hand over the receiver, she called out, "I'll be there soon, Meeko."

"You said that last time," answered the little voice.

For a moment everything was quiet. Krista cradled the phone on her shoulder and slid into a more comfortable position. Soon she forgot about Meeko.

A loud crash broke into Krista's conversation. She jumped up, filled with panic. *What happened?* she wondered as she quickly ended the phone call and ran for Meeko's bedroom.

No one there.

"Where are you, Meeko?" Krista called out. "Me-e-e-e-ko!"

In that instant Krista heard a little sound. Heading down the hall, she came to the master bedroom. As she tried to open the door, it stopped partway.

Looking down, Krista discovered the reason. A large piece from a glass lamp had spun across the hardwood floor. Other pieces lay all around one side of the bed. And on the bed sat Meeko, looking scared.

"Meeko, shame on you!" snapped Krista. "You're supposed to be in bed. What are you doing in here?"

Tears welled up in Meeko's eyes. "You didn't come when I called you." The tears started to slide down her cheeks. "I want my mommy."

Krista looked at Meeko, then at the floor. *I'm in big trouble*, she thought. *What am I gonna tell her mom and dad?*

Then another thought struck Krista. *Meeko must have pushed the lamp off the bedside table. What if she'd been on the floor and* pulled *it off?* It wasn't hard to imagine the little girl all cut up from flying glass.

Krista didn't want to face the truth, yet it hit her like a bolt of lightning. *It was really my fault, wasn't it, God?* In that moment Krista didn't like herself very much.

Going around to the side clear of glass, Krista crawled onto the bed and picked up Meeko. With the little girl in her arms, Krista carried her to the living room.

Sitting down in a big rocker, Krista tried to comfort Meeko. But the little girl's sobs increased.

Just then the phone jangled. "We've been trying to reach you for over an hour," said Mrs. Perry. "We couldn't get through because of the busy signal. Is everything okay?"

For a moment Krista wanted to lie and pretend nothing had happened. She wanted to act as if it were all Meeko's fault. But as she opened her mouth to make excuses, something made her stop.

In that instant Krista knew she had to make a choice. *Am I going to be honest about what happened?*

Krista took a deep breath. "We've had a problem here,"

she said. "But I'm taking care of it. I'll tell you about it when you get home."

"You're sure?" asked Mrs. Perry.

"I'm sure," Krista said. "We're doing fine now."

As she hung up the phone, Krista made another choice—a promise to herself and to God. "I'm going to be different."

TO **TALK** ABOUT

▸ What do you think Krista should tell Mr. and Mrs. Perry when they come home? It would be easy for Krista to make up excuses or lie about what happened. Why is it important for Krista's own sake that she doesn't?

▸ Krista wants to be someone others can count on and trust. What habits will she need to break in order to keep her promise to herself and to God?

▸ Do you baby-sit, either at home or in someone else's house? What are some ideas you could give Krista to help her become a better baby-sitter?

▸ Sometimes baby-sitting seems like a boring job that can be done any way you want. Yet your relationships with the children you baby-sit can be some of the most important relationships you have. Whether you're a boy or a girl, how can your baby-sitting experience help you as you grow older?

▸ People who hire grown-ups for a job often say, "I want to hire a person with integrity." There's a test for whether you have integrity. **Integrity is doing the right thing when no one except you and God know.** How can

God help you have integrity? If you ask for His help, do you still need to make your own choices? Why or why not?

[Jesus said,] "You have been faithful with a few things; I will put you in charge of many things." Matthew 25:21

Lord, I want to be faithful to you. I want to be a person other people can count on. When I baby-sit, help me keep the children safe. Help me love them the way you do.

He's a Great Dad, But . . .

Cody slammed the car door, then remembered his manners and opened it again. "Thanks, Mr. Nilson. Thanks for taking me to the fair."

As Cody thought about it, he decided his time with Alan and Mr. Nilson had been one of the greatest days ever. *I wish I had a dad like that,* Cody thought.

The next morning at school he told Alan so. "What's it like to have such a totally awesome dad?"

For a moment Alan didn't answer. "Uh, okay, I guess," he finally said.

"What do you mean, okay? That's all you can say? Alan, he knew the best jokes."

"Yeah, sure."

"And it was fun going on the rides and doing things together."

"Sure, Cody," said Alan. "Hey, are you going out for football this year?"

Cody wondered if Alan wanted to change the subject, but he was afraid to ask why. Yet he kept thinking about it. *Alan's lucky to live with his dad. Why doesn't he say more about him?*

The week passed quickly, and on Friday afternoon Cody

started looking for something to do. After school he found Alan. "Let's go over to your house for a while."

"Not tonight," Alan told him.

"Well, how about tomorrow?" asked Cody.

"Nah, I'm gonna be busy."

"With what?" asked Cody.

"Oh, things. I'll see you Monday, okay?"

Monday came, then one week after another. Each time Cody suggested they go to Alan's, Alan always had an excuse. "Let's go to your place instead." Or, "Sorry, but Dad has something planned."

Finally one day Cody asked, "Hey, what's going on? I liked going to the fair with you and your dad. Don't you want me to come over? Is there something wrong with me?"

"Nah," said Alan. "Dad's just busy."

"I think he's the greatest. I'd like to see him again—and talk with him."

"Well, sometime." Alan let it slide.

The next Saturday Cody wanted something to do. *I'm tired of Alan's excuses*, he thought. *I'm going over there. Maybe Mr. Nilson's mad at me, and Alan's afraid to tell me.*

Half an hour later, Cody pounded on the back door. After a long wait, Mr. Nilson came to the door with a drink in his hand. "Yeah, kid, whadd'ya want?" The words slurred as he spoke.

"Is Alan around?" Cody asked.

"Nah, whadd'ya need him for?" Again the words slid around in Mr. Nilson's mouth.

A sick feeling clutched the pit of Cody's stomach. "Uh, just to do something with. Where is he?"

"Hey, kid, do you think all I have ta do is answer your questions?"

Unable to believe his ears, Cody stared at Mr. Nilson. He wanted to say, "I'm Cody, remember? You took me to the fair. You showed me a good time." But his tongue refused to move.

The sick feeling in his stomach changed to panic. *How can he forget who I am?*

Just then Alan came up behind his dad. "What's going on?"

In that moment, Alan caught sight of Cody, and his face flushed red. "Hi, Cody," he said as though he wished his friend weren't there.

"Hi, Alan," answered Cody, trying to pretend nothing was wrong. "Just wanted to see if you can do something this afternoon." Even as he spoke, his words sounded strange and stiff.

"Not right now," Alan said, his voice as strange as Cody's. "See you around, okay?"

Cody looked at Alan, then at Mr. Nilson. As Cody stood there, the door closed in his face. Cody stared at it. *How can Mr. Nilson be so different? When he took us to the fair, was he just having a good day?*

Slowly Cody started down the steps. *What will I do when I see Alan again? Do I talk about his dad? Or pretend there's nothing wrong?*

TO **TALK** ABOUT

▸ Sometimes people say, "The grass is greener on the other side of the fence." What do those words mean? Why did Cody think Alan had a better home life?

‣ Why did Mr. Nilson seem like two different people? What do you believe is his real problem?

‣ Why do you think Alan didn't want Cody to know about his dad's drinking? How would it help Alan to talk to Cody about his dad?

‣ What do you think Cody should do the next time he sees Alan? If Alan doesn't bring up the problem, should Cody talk about it, or pretend nothing happened? Why?

‣ **It takes courage to help a friend who's afraid to tell you what's wrong. Yet a good friend listens and cares.** What's the difference between being nosy and showing you care? If you were Cody, what would you say to Alan?

‣ Why is it important that Alan and Cody go together to talk with an adult? Who are some adults who could help?

‣ **When Jesus faced a problem, He did not ignore it.** Instead, He spoke up and chose a good way to correct the problem. **Jesus also showed compassion to people who suffered.** What does it mean to show compassion? In what ways can you show compassion to a friend who is having a difficult time?

Friends always show their love. What are relatives for if not to share trouble? Proverbs 17:17 (TEV)

Jesus, I often feel that others are better off than I am. If one of my friends is having a hard time, help me know what to do. Give me the ability to listen, and help, and talk to a grown-up when I should.

100

Backyard Discovery

"Want some cookies?" asked Lucas, digging deep into the jar.

Gino was his best friend and had come home with Lucas from school. As they downed cookies and milk, they tried to decide what to do.

Just then Matt joined them at the kitchen table. Older by three years, he was also five inches taller than Lucas. "How about shooting baskets?" he asked.

Lucas knew what that would be like. His big brother was a great basketball player. "Nah," Lucas answered. "Let's not."

But Gino was interested. When Matt said, "I'll give you some tips," it was decided.

Slowly Lucas stood up and followed them out to the hoop in front of the garage. *Why does Matt do this? Gino's my friend, but Matt takes over.*

"I'll start by shooting a basket from here," Matt said as he stood directly in front of the hoop. "You try next, Gino. If you make a basket from the same position, you get the point. If not, I get the point."

Matt's shot swished through the net. Gino stood in the same place, and his ball also dropped through.

"Good! The point's yours," Matt said. "Now stand wherever you want. If you put it in, Lucas tries from the same spot."

Gino moved over to one side and ran in for a lay-up. Sure enough, he made the basket. But when Lucas tried the same shot, the ball hit the hoop and bounced off.

Soon they'd each had several turns. With every shot, Lucas tried harder. Yet his score stayed at zero while Matt's jumped ahead.

I can't keep up! thought Lucas. *I can't even keep up with Gino.* As the gap between their scores and his widened, Lucas felt embarrassed. Then he started feeling like a failure.

I can't do anything *as well as Matt*, Lucas decided. The more hopeless he felt, the more Matt and Gino seemed to enjoy the game.

"Here, do it this way," Matt would say to Gino. "You'll get a better shot." But usually Matt forgot to help Lucas. Or if he tried, Lucas couldn't do what he said.

"Hey, let's do something else," Lucas told Gino.

But Gino wanted to keep on. Finally Lucas gave up and dropped down on the nearby grass. His brother and friend didn't seem to notice.

I can't stand Matt! Lucas decided. *He's always stealing my friends.*

For a while Lucas sat there watching Matt and Gino shoot baskets and growing more discouraged by the minute. *I'll never be as good*, Lucas told himself. *I won't even try.*

After a time, Lucas noticed something had changed in the way Gino played. He was dropping in still more shots. *Maybe Matt really helped him*, thought Lucas. *And Gino cares more about basketball than I do.*

As Gino's next long shot swished through the net, Lucas forgot about himself. "Good one!"

Gino looked over and grinned. For the first time Matt seemed to notice that Lucas had dropped out.

"Come here," Matt told him. "I'll show you how, too."

Slowly Lucas stood up. *I'll never be as good. But I don't have to wreck Gino's fun. Guess I better make the best of it.*

Ten minutes later Lucas discovered something. When he stopped trying so hard, he started having fun.

But his biggest surprise came when he sank a basket after a new play. Matt clapped him on the back and said, "Hey, that's really great!"

Lucas felt great on the inside, too.

TO **TALK** ABOUT

▸ Whenever Lucas was around Matt, he asked himself, "How am I doing *compared* to Matt?" Why did that question make Lucas feel he was failing?

▸ How did family position affect what Lucas thought he could do?

▸ Why do you think Lucas did better when he stopped trying so hard?

▸ Lucas needs to make some choices. He can
  1) wait until Gino goes home and tell his brother to leave his friend alone;
  2) learn from Matt and try to become a good basketball player; or
  3) try to excel in a different area—one where he doesn't

have to compete with Matt.

What do you think Lucas should do? Why?

▸ If Lucas chooses to work at basketball, why might he become a better player than other kids his age?

▸ What happened when Lucas forgot about himself and encouraged Gino?

▸ What does it mean to feel pushed beyond what you can handle? What does it mean to be gifted in some way? It's great to be a good player, but even if you aren't, you can have fun in a sport. Many kids aren't good in competitive sports but enjoy something like in-line skating or family bicycling trips. What are some sports that offer great exercise without big competition?

▸ Have you discovered activities other than sports that you enjoy? Think about all the things you can do in music, for instance. These can become lifetime interests. What *is* a lifetime interest? **Ask Jesus to give you some really special lifetime interests.**

I was pushed back and about to fall, but the Lord helped me.
Psalm 118:13

Show me, Jesus, when I should try to get better at something, and when I should learn to grow in a different way. Help me find activities I can enjoy doing and even do well. But also help me to encourage other kids in what they can do.

On Eagles' Wings

It seemed the February day would never end. Chip's science report on bald eagles had been a disaster—his classmates snickered all the way through. Though Chip could have talked much longer, he sat down without finishing.

Lunch time wasn't any better. There Chip got in a fight. But finally he was on the bus going home. When it ground to a halt, he and his friend Rob climbed down together. Chip's house was at the end of a long dirt road back in the woods. Rob's family lived on the same road, but closer to the highway.

Sometimes Rob seemed like Chip's best buddy. Other times Chip couldn't stand him. Today their fight started the minute they got off the bus.

"Why didn't you back me up?" Chip asked as they talked about what had happened during lunch hour. "You could have told the teacher that it wasn't my fault."

"But it was," Rob said. "You picked on Tommy, and I'm not gonna lie about it."

Chip felt unwilling to tell Rob that he had beaten up Tommy because he laughed at him. "It wasn't my fault," Chip said instead.

"Oh yeah? Like it wasn't your fault when you went squirrel hunting and shot the windows out of old man Bailey's barn."

Chip bent down, picked up some snow, and started shaping a ball.

"Like it wasn't your fault that you swiped a can of gas last night."

Suddenly Chip looked up.

"Saw you comin' out of our shed," Rob said. "I was upstairs and it was dark, but I just happened to look out. Why'd you want it, anyway? Were you going snowmobiling?"

Chip bent down for more snow.

"If you'd asked, Mom would've given it to you. Why didn't you ask?"

Chip shrugged. Sure, he should have asked. Sometimes he just didn't think things through. Instead, he stumbled into trouble. But right now he didn't want Rob telling on him. It wouldn't be so bad if Rob was just good in school. He was good in *everything*. He could hunt and fish and trap, and even play the guitar.

More than once Chip had given him a bloody nose to set things straight between them. Now Chip felt uneasy. *If Rob tells his mom, she'll tell my mom. Maybe I should beat Rob up, just to make sure he doesn't.*

As though reading Chip's thoughts, Rob started running and stayed out of Chip's reach. When Chip lobbed a snowball in his direction, Rob ducked and headed into his yard. When Rob's mom looked out the kitchen window, Chip knew better than to try again.

Walking on, he soon left the dirt road. The snow was still deep in the woods, but Chip followed a deer path. During the winter this was the best part of the day—being set free from that stuffy old room at school.

Before long, Chip came to a rise that gave him a good view. Below, the swiftly moving water of a small river emptied into a lake. Nearby, a tall white pine held a bald eagles' nest.

Chip stood without moving, filled with the excitement the huge nest always gave him. Finally his wait was rewarded. High above, two eagles soared against the winter sky.

In that moment something soared within Chip. *I don't need dumb old school,* he decided. *Why should I study all that stuff?*

For Chip, school was hard. Sure, he could do the work if he wanted. He just didn't care. Lately he'd been telling himself he didn't care what people thought about him, either. But the last time he'd gotten in trouble at school, Mom started crying.

As Chip remembered her face, he didn't feel good. Then he pushed his feelings aside, shrugged his shoulders, and grinned. At least there were a lot of things his mom *didn't* know. Just the same, Chip still wondered if Rob would tell on him.

After supper Chip was in his bedroom when Rob's mom came over. From the sound of her voice, she and Mom were sitting at the kitchen table, drinking coffee. Usually they were good friends, but in the last few months there had been trouble between them—trouble Chip had caused.

Quietly he opened his door a crack and listened. Now and then he picked out his name and some words—playground, principal, trouble.

"Today I was missing a can of gas," said Rob's mom, her voice a bit louder. "I asked Rob about it, and he said . . ."

Mom's answer sounded angry. "How do you know Rob's telling the truth?"

For a moment there was an awful quiet. When Rob's mom broke the stillness, her voice came clear and cold. "Your kid will never amount to anything."

Chip stepped away from the door. Anger boiled up within him. *That old lady telling Mom a thing like that!* Wanting to fly out of the room and yell at Rob's mom, Chip clenched his fists. As the fire of anger raced through him, there was nothing he wanted more than a rip-roaring fight.

I'll get even with that jerk Rob! he thought. *He'll never tell on me again!*

But then Chip had an awful thought. *What if Rob's mom is right? What if I* don't *amount to anything?*

Chip slid to the floor and sat with his back against the wall. Soon he heard Rob's mom get up and leave. Still he sat on the floor, the room dark around him.

Maybe she's right, Chip thought. Pictures flashed in his mind of the times he'd gotten in trouble. All the times he'd been caught. And all the times he'd done something wrong and gotten away with it. For a long time Chip sat there, just thinking.

The next afternoon on the way home from school, Chip swung past the eagles' nest again. As he watched, an eagle with a small branch in his large yellow beak swooped down. Chip waited, and before long the other eagle returned to add new twigs to the nest.

Chip felt something stir within him—something that wanted to soar as the eagles did. For the first time in many months he felt hope. For the first time in his life he promised himself something important. *I'm gonna prove Rob's mom is wrong. I'm gonna make something of myself!*

That afternoon Chip returned the can of gas and apologized. Rob's mom looked surprised, but just said thanks.

The next morning Chip began listening in class.

He had looked out the window for so long that it was hard work. Often he didn't feel like trying, but then he remembered the eagles. As the days went on, he began to understand more of what the teacher said.

It was hardest to stop fighting. The kids at school still looked for reasons to poke fun at him. Often Chip clenched his fists to hold himself back. More than once he wanted to beat up on someone.

But he and Rob were friends again, and Rob told him, "Just pretend you don't see what they're doing." After that, Chip started getting along with the kids on the playground.

One day he had a thought he wouldn't tell even Rob. *Maybe it's good Rob's mom said what she did.* Chip had to admit things were going better.

Off and on, Chip watched the eagles from a distance. One morning in May he knew the babies had hatched. The adult eagles flew back and forth, carrying fish and other food in their beaks.

I better get Rob, Chip thought. *He'll wanna see 'em, too.* It felt good to be buddies again.

Around Chip the woods had come alive with the sounds of spring. Inside, he felt himself stretching up, up, up. In his own way he would soar.

TO **TALK** ABOUT

▸ How did the kids at school treat Chip? How did he feel about himself?

▸ When Chip got in trouble, how did it affect his relationship with Rob? How did it affect the relationship between the two mothers?

▶ Why did Chip *like* Rob? Why did Chip *dislike* him? What made the difference in how Chip felt about Rob at the end of the story?

▶ It would be easy for Chip to think, *Nobody likes me. People have been so mean to me that I'm gonna give up.* Instead, what was the turning point in Chip's life?

▶ How did that turning point make a change in Chip's thinking and the way he acted? Why was it hard for him to change?

▶ **Sometimes God uses the hard things in our lives to help us change. But we are the ones who make the choices about what we're going to do.** What hard things have happened to you? What did you do to face those times?

▶ When Chip started to change, he began using all the ability God had given him. In what ways would you like to grow and use all of your ability? In what ways can the Holy Spirit give you the power to change?

Help me, Jesus, to be honest with myself about where I'm at. Thank you that if I'm honest, you can turn the hard things in my life into something good. Give me the Holy Spirit's power to help me become the person you want me to be.

[The Lord said,] "I carried you on eagles' wings and brought you to myself." Exodus 19:4b

Runaway Secret

When Alyssa stayed overnight with Holly, they talked and giggled all evening long. Now it was late. As they stretched out on their sleeping bags, Holly had a question.

"Alyssa, do you tell me all your secrets?"

Alyssa thought for a moment. "Wel-l-l-l—"

"Well, you should," Holly said. "After all, we're really good friends."

Alyssa was quiet, not sure she wanted to tell Holly everything she thought and felt.

But Holly kept on. "When I tell you a secret, I know you won't tell anyone. And I wouldn't tell anyone your secrets."

"You're sure?" asked Alyssa.

"For *sure*," answered Holly. "I wouldn't give away a secret for *anything*. Especially a secret that's yours."

Alyssa still felt uneasy. What if Holly didn't understand?

Holly rolled over onto her stomach. "I've told you all my secrets. Why haven't you told me yours?"

Alyssa's secret was so special that she didn't want to tell anyone. Talking about it might spoil the special way she felt.

"Come on, Alyssa. That's what friends are for!"

Can I really count on you? Alyssa wondered.

"I promise not to tell a soul," said Holly, as though reading Alyssa's thoughts.

"Promise?" asked Alyssa.

"Promise," answered Holly, her brown eyes serious.

So Alyssa told Holly about how much she liked Jordan. She told Holly how special Jordan acted whenever she saw him at school and how cute he was when he smiled. And how maybe—just maybe—he liked her.

"You won't tell anyone? You promise?" asked Alyssa.

"I said *promise*, didn't I?" said Holly. "Your secret's safe with me."

Soon after, they fell asleep. The next morning Alyssa wondered if she'd done the right thing in telling Holly her secret. *But I can trust her*, Alyssa decided. *After all, we're best friends.*

Two days later Alyssa started to worry. As she walked down the hall at school, she saw three girls in a huddle, talking and giggling.

Seeing Alyssa, they stopped talking. As if a thin sliver of light shone through a window, Alyssa felt uneasy deep inside.

Later that day she knew for sure. When she ran outside for gym, the other girls started teasing her.

"Alyssa loves Jordan! Alyssa loves Jordan!" In a singsong chant the words rose all around her.

Alyssa's face grew hot with embarrassment. She tried to pretend she didn't hear. But the girls kept chanting, their voices growing louder all the time.

What if Jordan hears them? In panic Alyssa looked around to see where the boys were. Sure enough, Jordan was far down the field, playing soccer. As Alyssa watched, his team took a time out.

"Shhhhhh!" Alyssa begged. "Be quiet! He'll hear you!"

But the girls chanted louder, and Jordan turned in their direction.

Alyssa wished she could be a turtle and crawl inside a shell. She ached now, ached with the hurt of it. *I'll never be able to look Jordan in the face again.*

As soon as school was over, Alyssa hunted down Holly. "You said you were my best friend!"

"I am!" answered Holly.

"And you spread it all over school that I like Jordan. I've never been more embarrassed in my life!"

"What? All over school? No, I didn't!"

"Yes, you did!"

"Says who?"

"Says me. How else could the whole school know?"

"You're kidding!" Holly looked upset. "Really?"

"Really."

"I only told one person. Samantha promised—"

"That she would never say a word?"

"Oh, Alyssa! I'm so sorry! I really, really am. Will you forgive me?"

But Alyssa wasn't ready to forgive. "Holly, you promised. And now you just say two little words—I'm sorry. I'm left with all the mess. Forever and ever!"

Holly's brown eyes filled with tears. "Alyssa, I really am sorry. I'm sorry I told. I'm sorry I hurt you."

Alyssa glared at her. *What should I say?* she wondered. *Can I ever count on Holly again?*

TO **TALK** ABOUT

▸ Why is it hard to keep a secret? Why do most of us feel more important if we have a secret to tell?

▸ What does it mean to trust someone? How did Alyssa trust Holly? How did Holly destroy Alyssa's trust in her?

▸ Do you think Alyssa should forgive Holly? Why or why not?

▸ In what way could Alyssa show her love to Holly by giving her a second chance? Do you think she should? Give reasons for your answer.

▸ Do you think Alyssa should ever tell Holly another secret? Why or why not?

▸ If we lose trust in someone, why is it hard to believe in that person again?

▸ Some secrets are different from the kind that Holly told. Some secrets are not meant to be kept. When is it important to tell a parent or another adult a secret between kids? Why might talking at that time keep someone from getting hurt?

▸ What does it mean to share *good* things with our friends? **Each time we pray to Jesus, we can trust Him with our lives, thoughts, feelings, and all that we are.** Why is He worthy of our trust?

[Jesus said,] "I call you friends, because I have told you everything I heard from my Father. You did not choose me; I chose you and appointed you to go and bear much fruit, the kind of fruit that endures." John 15:15b–16 (TEV)

Thank you, Jesus, that I can pray to you, my best Friend, whenever I want. Help me to be a true friend—a person others can trust. When I need to forgive someone, remind me of how often you have forgiven me. But also help me know whether it's okay to put my trust in someone.

Tagalong Trudy

As Jessica brushed her hair, she caught a movement in the mirror. Her little sister stood right behind her. Wobbling forward on tiptoes, Trudy tried to see herself. Turning this way and that, she managed to brush her hair just the way Jessica did hers.

Jessica groaned. *Will it never end?* she asked herself. *Whatever I do, Trudy wants to do it, too. Well, at least she can't tag along to the slumber party tonight.*

As soon as Jessica finished breakfast, she tried to sneak out. Maybe she could meet her friend Amber at the tennis courts without having Trudy along.

But Trudy guessed where Jessica was headed. "Can I go, too?" she asked Mom.

"Well, you can't go by yourself," Mom answered. "Will you take her, Jessica? And see that she gets home okay?"

"Aw, Mom! Does Trudy always have to tag along?"

"She can play with her friends while you play with yours."

To Jessica's surprise it wasn't as bad as she thought. While she played tennis, Trudy found some girls her age on the nearby monkey bars.

A few hours later Jessica started home. As she and her friend Amber walked together, Trudy fell behind. Wondering what had happened to her, Jessica turned around. Trudy had her head down, as if she were looking for invisible footprints. What on earth was she doing?

"What's the matter?" Amber asked, and Jessica shrugged her shoulders.

Soon she felt curious and glanced back again. Trudy still walked strangely. Stretching out her legs, she took much bigger strides than usual. *Aha!* thought Jessica. *She's trying to walk in my footsteps!*

When Jessica started walking as fast as she could, Amber looked at her. "What are you doing?"

Jessica put her finger to her lips, whispered, "Shh," and tipped her head backward.

Amber looked at Trudy and grinned. She, too, began walking in long, giant strides. Still trying to stay in Jessica's steps, Trudy started running. Soon she was gasping for breath.

Jessica stopped, ready to say, "You're sure acting stupid, Trudy." But something inside Jessica made her hold back the words. *Does she really care that much about being like me? Even in the way I walk?*

Seconds later Jessica was glad she hadn't said anything. As Amber turned off for her own house, Trudy reached out for Jessica's hand.

Jessica looked down. For the first time she caught a glimpse of how much her little sister loved her. *It's kind of scary*, Jessica thought. *What if I do something to hurt her?* Somehow Trudy wasn't just a tagalong anymore.

When Jessica and Trudy reached home, Mom met them in the kitchen. "I have a problem. Your dad and I are supposed to go to a concert tonight. Our baby-sitter just canceled. Do you know anyone who won't be going to your slumber party?"

Jessica thought for a minute, then shook her head.

"I know what you can do with me," Trudy said. "I can go to Amber's slumber party!"

"Mo-o-o-mmm!" Jessica cried out. In that moment all of her good feelings about Trudy disappeared.

Then, as though she were seeing a video, Jessica remembered Trudy trying to walk in her footsteps. Instead of blurting out her feelings, Jessica waited until her little sister went into the bathroom.

The moment the door shut, Jessica drew a deep breath and plunged in, telling Mom how she felt.

TO TALK ABOUT

▸ Thought*less*ness tears relationships down. Thought*ful*ness builds them up. What are some thoughtful things Jessica did in handling Trudy?

▸ When you live in a family, you sometimes need to give in and think about another person. Other times you need to explain why you feel the way you do. Which kind of time is this for Jessica?

▸ When Jessica explains how she feels about Trudy tagging along, she should tell two things: 1) what the problem is, and 2) how she feels about the problem. Pretend you're Jessica. What would you say to your mom?

▸ Whose idea was it for Trudy to go to the slumber party? What's the difference between Jessica taking Trudy to the park and taking her to a slumber party?

‣ How would her friends feel about inviting Jessica if she always took Trudy along?

‣ When you tell how you feel about something that happens in your family, you help your mom or dad understand things they may not have thought about. It also helps you feel better because you get your feelings out in the open. **Often things don't seem as hard if you talk about them with the right person.** What problems are you facing now that you'd like to talk about? A good way to begin is by saying, "I feel . . ." Then finish the sentence, using feeling words like *angry* or *sad* or *glad*. If you have ideas for solving your problem, be sure to mention them.

‣ **Besides talking with the right human being, you can talk with Jesus whenever you want.** What are some words you can use to begin?

Love each other with brotherly affection and take delight in honoring each other. Romans 12:10 (TLB)

Help me, Jesus, to be thoughtful about the feelings of others. Help me know when I should help someone else, and when I should explain what I need. Help our family to have good talks together.

Hometown Hero

As Joel and his friend Ben watched TV, Dad called from outside.

"Five more minutes, Dad," Joel answered. "Okay?"

But as the program ended, a news flash caught and held him.

"Major league football player arrested for illegal possession of drugs. Arrested outside his home this morning, starting quarterback . . ."

Joel jumped up, feeling like someone had kicked him in the stomach. "I don't believe it!"

But the newscaster went on, giving more details, then ending, "Update at five."

"That's awful!" Joel said. "I can't believe such a good player would do drugs."

"Hey, what's with you?" answered Ben. "Everybody's doing it."

"That's not true!"

"Sure it is! What's the big deal? My brother does." Suddenly Ben stopped, as though remembering he wasn't supposed to say anything.

Joel turned off the TV. Ben headed home, and Joel went out to the backyard. His feet dragged the entire way.

When Joel joined him, Dad dropped a large log onto the wood splitter. Joel stood across from him and threw off the pieces that were the right size. When they needed to be split again, he pushed them back in against the wedge.

The woodpile grew higher, but Joel's mind wasn't on his work. The first time he let half a log fall off, Dad didn't say anything. The second time it happened, Joel caught Dad looking at him.

After that, Joel tried to think about what he was doing. Just the same, it wasn't long before he bumped a finger.

"Ow, ow, ow!" Pulling off his glove, Joel sucked the finger.

Dad stopped the splitter and sat down on a stump. "What's the matter, Joel? Besides your finger, I mean."

Joel dropped down on the ground. "Aw, nothing." But he turned away from Dad.

"Sure there is. Why don't you tell me about it?"

As Joel thought about the news flash, he felt kicked in the stomach again. It upset him so much that he didn't think he could tell Dad about it.

But Dad asked a second time. In spite of his hurt, Joel found himself talking about the football player. "Ben thinks it's okay—that practically everybody does drugs. But this guy was my hero! I've always looked up to him. I thought he was different!"

Joel's anger spilled out. "He even came from our town! When I was a little kid, he autographed my football."

"And you've had it on your shelf ever since. It hurts, doesn't it?"

Joel felt the tears at the back of his eyes and was glad Dad couldn't see his face.

"You believed in him," Dad went on. "He made it to the big time."

Joel felt surprised that Dad understood. "I wanted—someday I wanted—" Joel broke off, afraid he'd sound—well, crazy, for dreaming big.

But Dad guessed. "You wanted to be like him when you grow up."

Joel nodded, still trying to hold back the tears. Instead, they began streaming down his cheeks. Feeling embarrassed, Joel struggled to speak. "He was my hero—my hometown hero. . . ."

Dad reached out and put his arm around Joel's shoulders. "We need to be able to believe in people. But often they disappoint us, especially if we think they're perfect."

Joel pulled up the edge of his jacket and wiped his face. "He was like one of us. If I can't believe in him, who can I trust?"

"It hurts me, too, Joel. I feel disappointed and angry. I also feel concerned for him. I wonder what happened that a football player with all he had going for him decided to try something that would hurt him."

Dad squeezed Joel's shoulder. "When I was about your age, a singer I especially liked disappointed me."

As if the memory still hurt, Dad spoke quietly. "Because a sports hero or political figure or *any* well-known person chooses to do something wrong, it doesn't make it right."

Dad cleared his throat. "Later on, something happened that bothered me even more. Maybe it sounds silly, but it wasn't to me. My grandpa promised to take me fishing. I looked forward to it all week. I told all the kids at school. But Gramps got busy and forgot."

Something in Dad's voice caught Joel's attention. Joel turned to face him.

Dad took a deep breath. "And even though I don't want

to, maybe I'll disappoint you someday, too."

"But you're trying your best to be a good dad," Joel said. "And the football player was my idol."

"Your idol?"

"Yeah, my idol."

"You need people you can respect, Joel. But it doesn't work to have idols. They might start meaning more to you than God."

After a long, quiet moment, Dad stood up. "There's only one Person who will never disappoint you."

Pulling on his work gloves, Joel stood up, too. He still hurt inside. Maybe he would for a long time. But he knew who that one Person was.

TO TALK ABOUT

▸ Why is it important that we have people we can look up to? How can they help us grow and reach out to do hard things?

▸ What mistake did Joel make in thinking about his hero?

▸ What is an idol? What are some idols that people have?

▸ Have you ever believed in someone and been badly disappointed? What happened?

▸ Joel's dad said, **"Because a sports hero or political figure or *any* well-known person chooses to do something wrong, it doesn't make it right."** What does that mean?

▸ **Each of us has a responsibility to people who like and respect us.** What does it mean to take responsibility?

▸ What if we do something wrong and are tempted to put the blame on someone else? Is that taking responsibility for what we do? Why or why not?

▸ Sometimes grandparents or other people try very hard to keep a promise and cannot because of poor health or another important reason. How can you help someone who does his best to keep a promise but can't?

▸ Who is the one Person Joel's dad talked about? Why is He the only person who will never disappoint you?

"Whoever believes in [Jesus] will not be disappointed." Romans 10:11 (TEV)

Jesus, I hurt inside when I like someone and find out that he or she isn't as great as I thought. Thanks that I can look to you, and you will never disappoint me. Make me strong. Help me to live in a way that I won't disappoint you or other people. Thanks for being my forever Friend.

We're the Best!

Tonya woke to a stream of sunlight coming through the window. For a moment she didn't know where she was. Then she remembered—Dad's new house.

In the other bed, Jodi still slept. *She'd be nice*, Tonya thought. *That is, if she didn't have to be my sister.*

Tonya wished there weren't a Jodi. She wished there weren't two younger brothers. Most of all, she wished there weren't Jodi's mom, Danielle.

Tonya closed her eyes and tried to go back to sleep. Instead, she remembered how she felt about leaving Mom for this weekend with Dad's new family.

"The divorce is something between Dad and me," Mom had told her. "I don't like it any more than you do. But he's your father. You can love me and still have a good relationship with him."

Instead, Tonya felt angry that there had been a divorce. She felt jealous that Jodi and her brothers got to be with Dad all the time. Even worse, Tonya felt lonely and afraid and wished Mom were here.

Are they going to leave me out? she wondered. *Or will they act nice to me because they think they have to?*

Jodi stirred, and the day began. Around the breakfast

table, Dad brought out new T-shirts he'd bought. They were bright red with bold blue letters across the front that said, WE'RE THE BUTTERFIELDS. Across the back were more words: WE'RE THE BEST!

Tonya looked at Jodi and could tell she liked the shirts. With a whoop, her two little brothers tore off the shirts they were wearing and pulled on the new ones. Danielle smiled at Dad, and Dad smiled back.

But Tonya felt terrible. She remembered when she was Dad's only kid. *Do I still count with him? Does he still love me?* she wondered. Then she thought of Mom sitting home alone. Wearing the shirt seemed disloyal to her.

"Let's get 'em on and go for a hike," Dad said.

Tonya jumped up, glad to get away from the table. But she moved slowly up the stairs. Even more slowly, she shut the door to the room she and Jodi shared.

Grateful that Jodi hadn't followed her, Tonya sat down on the floor. She felt mad and sad all at once.

I don't want to wear that stupid shirt. I'm not a Butterfield. Sure, that's my name. But I'm not part of this family.

For a long time she sat there, unwilling to move. Then someone knocked on the door. "Hey, Tonya!" Dad called out.

Tonya didn't answer, and Dad called again. Finally she stood up and opened the door.

"We're all ready. Let's go." Then Dad saw Tonya's face. "What's the matter?"

Tonya made herself look at Dad. "I don't want to wear the shirt you gave me."

Just in time she caught the hurt look in his eyes. "I've got a new life, Tonya," he said. "I want you to be part of it."

But Tonya looked down.

"You're worried about your mother, aren't you?"

Slowly Tonya nodded.

"Why don't we call this a special shirt? Wear it on weekends when you're with us. Just leave it here when you go home."

Still Tonya stared at the floor.

"I love you, Tonya," Dad said softly. "Because I have a new family doesn't mean I love you less. My love gets bigger to take in all of you."

Dad gave her a quick hug. As he headed for the stairs, he turned back. "You belong here, too, you know. We'll be waiting in the car for you."

When he left, Tonya picked up the shirt and looked once more at the lettering. With her finger she traced the B, then the U, then the whole name. "I love *you*, Mom," she whispered.

But then, as clearly as if Mom were there, Tonya remembered her words. *"He's your father. You can love me and still have a good relationship with him."*

Tonya turned over the shirt. Through the blur of tears, WE'RE THE BEST! stared up at her.

As Tonya blinked away her tears, she remembered Dad at the breakfast table. *I guess I have to think about his feelings, too.*

Tonya drew a deep breath. *Maybe I have to give up the idea of one family. Like it or not, I'm part of two families now.*

In that moment she made a choice. Slowly she pulled on the shirt. *Maybe someday I'll feel like I belong.*

TO **TALK** ABOUT

▶ What does it mean to be loyal to someone? Why is loyalty a good quality to have?

▶ Why did Tonya's feelings of loyalty make it hard for her when her parents were divorced? What idea helped her work out her problem?

▶ Because her dad had a new family, Tonya wondered if he still loved her. When a parent remarries, it may be difficult to see a mom or dad as often. Even though a dad or mom remarries, it doesn't change the love they have for their other children. How do you know Tonya's father loves her?

▶ Who is with Tonya no matter where she lives? How do you know?

▶ **In your daily life you can make countless choices about what happens to you. But it's not possible to control *everything* that happens to you. You especially can't control what grown-ups decide or how they act.** In times like that, what counts is what you do about the hard things you can't change. In what way do you need to know that God is with you? How can He help you with your problems?

▶ In what way can Jesus be Tonya's forever Friend?

[The Lord said,] "So do not fear, for I am with you; do not be dismayed, for I am your God. I will strengthen you and help you; I will uphold you with my righteous right hand." Isaiah 41:10

Thank you, God, for the parents you've given me. Show me how to have a good relationship with both of them. Thank you that wherever I live, you are with me.

Buffy and the Game

When Mom started a new job with different hours, Ryan didn't like it one bit. Now he had to do all kinds of things he never did before.

"Be sure to take Buffy out before you go to school," Mom said as she left for work.

"Aw, Mom," Ryan answered. "Have Jared do it. He's older."

"I've asked Jared to do other things. You're in charge of Buffy."

Usually Ryan liked the little cocker spaniel. He had taught her to fetch sticks, speak for a treat, play dead, and hold out a paw to shake hands. Whenever Ryan came home from school, Buffy waited at the door, wagging her tail in welcome.

Often she seemed to sense if Ryan was happy or sad. Once he was sick for two weeks and couldn't stand being in his room any longer. With a little help from Ryan, Buffy jumped up on the bed. Rolling over on the spread, she played dead. Then she tipped her head from side to side, seeming to talk with Ryan until he laughed.

But now Ryan was older. He had plenty of other things to do. Sometimes Buffy seemed like too much work.

Taking hold of her collar, Ryan opened the back door. As he hooked the collar to the long chain, a blast of cold air whipped through his hair. Ryan shivered and shut the door. Going into the family room, he plopped down in front of the TV.

As he caught the sports news, he called out to Jared, "Hey! Our hockey team won!"

Jared stuck his head in the door. "I know. And Dad bought tickets for tomorrow night's game!"

"For all of us?" asked Ryan. Hockey was his favorite sport.

"Yup. All of us."

Twenty minutes later Jared looked in on Ryan. "Aren't you ready?" He zipped up his jacket. "I'm going. I don't want to miss the bus."

Ryan jumped up, grabbed his books and jacket, and headed out the front door. As he ran after Jared, the winter air stung his cheeks. The bus was half a block away, but he made it.

When Ryan and Jared returned home that afternoon, something felt strange. At first the house just seemed quieter than usual. But as Ryan and Jared headed to the kitchen for peanut butter toast, Buffy barked.

"She's outside?" asked Jared. "You didn't bring her in?"

Ryan hurried to the back door. Buffy was so glad to see him that she jumped all over Ryan and licked his hands before bounding into the warm house. Feeling guilty, Ryan rolled on the floor, playing with her.

But Jared was angry. "She's a house dog. She's not used to being outside all day."

"Nothing happened," Ryan said quickly. "She's okay."

"If she lived in a doghouse, she'd have a thick coat,"

Jared went on. "But she hasn't. It's too cold to be outside so long."

"Hey, forget it!"

"She probably barked all day."

"I said, forget it!" snapped Ryan.

"No, I won't! I'm gonna tell Mom when she gets home."

"You do, and I'll say it's all your fault. You didn't tell me it was almost time for the bus. That's why I forgot Buffy."

"I'm not *supposed* to tell you when it's time for the bus," Jared answered. "You can read the clock."

All evening long the little dog shivered. When Ryan went to bed, he covered Buffy with a blanket and hoped Mom wouldn't notice. But the next morning Buffy's eyes were matted. Every now and then she wheezed. As she looked at Ryan, she whimpered.

Ryan felt scared, yet he wondered, *How can I pin the blame on Jared? If Mom and Dad find out, they'll ground me.*

"This dog is sick," said Mom at breakfast. "What happened?"

"It's Jared's fault," answered Ryan.

"No, it's not!" Jared said. "It's your fault, and you know it!"

"He's lying!" Ryan exclaimed. "I did some work for him, and he promised to take Buffy in."

Jared looked really angry now. "You're the liar! I can't believe the way you make up a story! You just don't want to get in trouble!"

Mom looked from one to the other. Ryan looked her straight in the eye.

Inside, he felt terrible. He knew he wasn't telling the truth. Yet if he explained what really happened, Mom wouldn't let him go to the hockey game.

Ryan leaned down and started petting Buffy.

TO **TALK** ABOUT

▸ How do you feel about what Ryan did to Buffy?

▸ When Ryan started doing something wrong, how did one thing build on top of another?

▸ What do you think Ryan's mom should say? Do you think Ryan will go to the game?

▸ What will happen to Ryan if he gets away with lying and blaming someone else when he's in trouble?

▸ Like a snowball rolled along the ground and getting bigger and bigger, Ryan's lie kept growing. How will his lie hurt his relationship with Jared?

▸ **When you lie, you choose between trying to keep something in the dark or bringing it into the light to deal with it.** If you've done something wrong, what's the best way to correct it? If you've lied about something, what's the best way to correct a lie? How do you know?

▸ **The test for whether you have integrity is what you do when no one but you and God know. Even if you are tempted to do something wrong, you can be trusted to do what is right.** Ryan can make a choice now—to keep lying or to be honest about what he did wrong. If a kid never stops lying, what happens when he or she grows up?

Think about what kind of future you want to build for yourself. Describe the kind of grown-up you want to be.

▸ Can you think of a time in which Jesus told a lie? Explain your answer. You'll find a big clue in John 14:6.

No temptation has seized you except what is common to man. And God is faithful; he will not let you be tempted beyond what you can bear. But when you are tempted, he will also provide a way out so that you can stand up under it.

1 Corinthians 10:13

Help me, Jesus, when I'm tempted to lie and put the blame on others. Through the power of your big name, I choose to tell the truth—to be honest with you, with others, and with myself. Thanks that you will give me the strength to tell the truth and live with integrity.

Whitney
Returns Home

"Your family wants me to go skiing with them?" Whitney asked.

"Sure," said Megan. "Why not?"

"I've never skied before. I don't know how."

"That doesn't matter," Megan answered. "We'll teach you. It's not hard to cross-country ski."

Inside, Whitney felt scared. *What if I can't do it?* But she kept pushing the thought aside. Every part of her wanted to try.

Aloud she asked, "You're *sure* your mom and dad want me along?"

"Yup. When we go for a weekend, they always let me take a friend. You're my first choice. Okay?"

"Okay!" But Whitney's thoughts raced off to her own family. *I can't imagine Mom and Dad wanting me along.* When they went somewhere, it was usually a bar or casino. They always left Whitney and her brother at home.

Megan broke into her thoughts. "We'll leave right after school on Friday and rent skis for you when we get there. Okay?"

"Okay," Whitney echoed again.

And so, it was all set. A week later Whitney, Megan, and

her mom and dad found an open space near the beginning of the ski trail.

"Slide your foot into place like this." Mrs. Sullivan showed Whitney how to put on her skis.

Mr. Sullivan explained the best way to move ahead. "You kick one ski backward and glide forward on the other."

Whitney tried it, and to her surprise she soon got the hang of it.

"Laura and I will take off first," said Mr. Sullivan. "We'll stop every now and then to make sure you're getting along okay." Jabbing their ski poles into the snow, Megan's mom and dad started down the trail.

"You're next," Megan said, and Whitney took her place at the top of the slight incline. "Just dig in your poles and push."

The winding trail led off through the woods. It wasn't long before Whitney felt at home on skis. She even managed the small hills without falling down very often. By the time she started getting tired, Whitney decided skiing was the most fun she'd ever had.

When she rounded a bend, she saw Megan's parents at the side of the trail. They'd brushed snow off a picnic table, and now Mrs. Sullivan took food from her backpack. "Winter picnic!" she called.

Whitney took off her skis and dropped onto the bench. As she saw the sandwiches and apples, her stomach growled. But just as she reached out, ready to dive in, every head bowed.

Every head except Whitney's. As Megan and her parents began praying, Whitney felt uncomfortable.

What a strange thing to do, she thought. Yet it seemed to mean something to them. Whitney closed her eyes so they wouldn't catch her staring. *Is that what makes them differ-ent?*

When everyone started skiing again, Whitney asked Megan, "How come your family has fun together?"

"What do you mean?"

"You're different."

Megan laughed, as though she wasn't sure how to take Whitney's words. "We're different, all right."

"You are. You're nice to each other. How come?"

Megan's grin faded, and her eyes were serious. "We haven't always been that way."

"What happened?"

"First Mom became a Christian. Then I did. Then we prayed for Dad. We prayed a lo-o-o-ng time."

As they followed the ski trail, Whitney was quiet, thinking about it. *Would that work with my family? They'd probably just laugh at the whole thing.*

When twilight fell on the woods, they stopped skiing. The next morning they began skiing again. Whitney still watched all the Sullivans. *I wish we could be like that.*

Deep inside Whitney a thought started to take shape. All day the longing grew inside her. She wanted something more in her life. She wanted more for her family.

Off and on, Whitney asked Megan questions. She discovered that Jesus loved her the way He loved the Sullivans. On Saturday night Whitney asked Jesus to be her Savior and Lord.

When the Sullivans took her home on Sunday afternoon, Whitney knew the hard part was ahead. *I want my family to know Jesus*, she thought. Yet she felt more scared than when she faced her first time on skis.

As she sat down for supper, Whitney looked around the

table. Her brother, Dustin, reached across for a roll. Mom helped herself to potatoes, and Dad lifted a fork to his mouth.

Wondering if they could hear the pounding of her heart, Whitney bowed her head. Silently she offered the prayer she had learned from the Sullivans.

When she looked up, Whitney saw Dustin staring at her. "What's with you?" he asked. "Did you get religion over the weekend?"

Whitney felt a warm flush reach her cheeks. "Yes, I did," she said quietly. She wondered if her heart could pound right out of her chest.

"So what are you, a Jesus freak or something?" asked Dustin, his voice scornful.

Then Mom jumped in. "Now, Whitney, we don't want you getting caught up in something that won't be good for you."

Whitney swallowed hard and wondered if she should bail out. *Should I pretend nothing happened to me? Will they ever understand?* Yet she knew she'd made a choice for something real.

Then Whitney saw the look in Dad's eyes. *He's listening,* she thought. *Maybe I'll have to pray for a long time, the way Megan and her mom did. But Dad is listening.*

In spite of the way Dustin poked fun at her, Whitney began to explain.

TO TALK ABOUT

▸ What made Whitney want what Megan's family had?

▸ Whitney learned about God by watching the Sullivans. What do you think Whitney told her family? Describe what you believe she said.

▸ What do you suppose would happen to Whitney's family if she didn't explain about how she received salvation?

▸ **Jesus promised that the Holy Spirit will be our Helper.** In what ways can the Holy Spirit help Whitney tell her family about Jesus? Explain.

▸ Has there been a time when the Holy Spirit helped you talk to someone who didn't know Jesus? What happened?

In what other ways can the Holy Spirit help you live your life? Big clue: Remember what Jesus said about the Holy Spirit. See John 14:15–16, 26.

[Jesus said,] "Go back home to your family and tell them how much the Lord has done for you and how kind he has been to you." Mark 5:19b (TEV)

Jesus, I'm often too scared to tell the people close to me about you. Yet I know you want me to speak up. In your name I ask for all the power of your Holy Spirit to help.

Thank you!

In the Middle of the Night

As Yuri ran down the alley, he felt the night press in. The footsteps behind him moved more quickly. Whoever was chasing him no longer tried to be quiet. Closer and closer the footsteps came.

With all the strength he had, Yuri rushed ahead. His heart pounded as loudly as the footsteps. If only he could reach home. If only he could get inside the door.

Somehow he had missed the way. Yuri looked around, searching for something he knew. Instead, the buildings on either side seemed to close in on him.

As he came to the end of the alley, he gasped. It was a dead end! He couldn't escape!

Just then Yuri felt a hand grab his shoulder. He hit out, trying to push the person away. Instead, the hand held on and kept shaking him. Then he heard a familiar voice.

"Yuri! Yuri! Wake up!"

As he opened his eyes, Yuri felt surprised. In the nightmare he'd been back in his own country. The old streets still seemed real. But now soft light streamed into his bedroom from the hallway. His new mom sat on the edge of the bed.

"What's the matter, Yuri?"

The night was still in his spirit, the alleyway too close. He was afraid to talk about it, afraid to admit how scared he'd been. "Nothing," he said.

"Yes, there is. Night after night you have terrible dreams. I don't think they'll stop until we talk about them."

But Yuri wasn't ready.

"Did you watch something scary on TV when we were gone this evening?"

Yuri shook his head.

"Did you read a scary book in school?"

Again Yuri shook his head. When he wouldn't talk, Mom kissed his forehead and returned to bed.

As soon as Yuri fell back asleep, he had another nightmare. He woke up moaning, then began sobbing. When Mom and Dad hurried into his room, Yuri tried to stop crying, but couldn't.

Dad sat down on one side of the bed and pulled Yuri close. "Something must have happened to you before you came to this country. Do you remember what it was?"

Slowly Yuri nodded as the tears streamed down his cheeks.

"Can you tell us about it?"

Yuri shook his head.

"Why don't you tell us what you're dreaming?" asked Mom.

"I can't remember it all," he answered, still afraid to admit how scared he felt.

"Just tell us what you do remember," said Dad. "Maybe you're having the same nightmare over and over."

It felt good to have Dad's arms around him. Yuri pulled up the quilt and settled deeper into bed. But he could barely get his words out.

"Someone always chases me. It's always dark. I keep trying to find our house, but I never can. It's never in the right place." Yuri's tears began again, and it was a long time before they stopped.

Finally Dad spoke. "Yuri, when you first came to our family, you didn't know enough English to tell us about your parents. Can you tell us now?"

Yuri's memory about his birth parents was buried so deep that he wasn't sure he could talk about it. But Dad waited, and finally Yuri said, "One day Mom and Dad were there. The next day they weren't. They left me."

In spite of Dad's arms and the blankets around him, Yuri shivered. "I cried and cried until someone came."

As Yuri looked up, he saw tears in Mom's eyes.

"That's why you're afraid, isn't it?" she asked. "That's why you keep having nightmares."

Yuri nodded, but there was something else. Yuri was afraid that if he said what was wrong, it might happen again.

Just the same, Mom guessed. "Yuri, are you afraid that something will happen to us? Are you afraid that we'll leave you?"

Yuri's gaze never left Mom's face, but finally he nodded.

Mom leaned forward and took Yuri's hand. "There's a verse in the Bible that says God puts those who are lonely in families [Psalm 68:6]. Let's ask God to help us take care of you. Okay?"

Yuri wasn't sure he wanted to be prayed for, but he knew his new mom and dad would do it anyway. In a secret place in his heart he felt glad. More than anything, he wanted to believe that the words in the Bible were true. When Mom and Dad bowed their heads, Yuri did, too.

"Jesus, help Yuri know that no matter what happens in his life, you will always take care of him," Dad began. "Give him the faith to believe what you've promised."

"And, Jesus, we ask you to heal Yuri," Mom prayed. "Fill him with your love, way down deep in his feelings and mind."

In that moment, something deep within Yuri reached up to Jesus. He couldn't explain it, but all of his hurt and scared feelings seemed to fall away. Deep inside, he felt peaceful.

Jesus, he thought. *Can the man named Jesus do that for me?*

Then Yuri spoke the name *Jesus* aloud. With all his heart, Yuri really wanted to know Him.

TO **TALK** ABOUT

▸ What does it mean to feel peaceful? Who has promised to give us peace? For a big clue, see John 14:27.

▸ When Jesus heals Yuri's mind and feelings, he will still remember that his birth parents were forced to leave him. But when Yuri thinks about it, he probably won't hurt in the same way. What do you suppose will happen to Yuri's nightmares? Why?

▸ Sometimes when we pray for someone, that person gets healed right away. Other times we need to pray many times for a person to be spiritually, emotionally, or physically healed. Do you think Yuri might need to be prayed for more than one time? Why or why not?

▸ Can you think of a time when Jesus helped you feel better about something that hurt or scared you? What happened? How did you know Jesus loves you? Explain what you mean.

▸ Both of Yuri's parents were forced to leave him. But some

children feel hurt because a mom or dad left home instead of staying married. Has that happened to you or someone you know? Why is it important to talk about your feelings with one or both of your parents?

▶ In what ways does God take care of you? Why can you always count on Jesus being with you?

Jesus promised that no matter what you face or what happens to you He will be with you. Memorize the promise that Jesus gives us about being our forever Friend: "Surely I will be with you always, to the very end of the age." Matthew 28:20

Thank you, Jesus, for your love for us. Thank you for your love for me. Thank you that you have promised to be with me always. In your strong name, Jesus, I ask you to heal me when I hurt. Thanks that I can always count on you.

The Real Winner

Captain for the Js, Janie crouched, ready for the jump. If there was anyone in the world she wanted to beat, it was Carla, captain of the Cs. No matter what Carla did, she always won. More than once they had played against each other. Janie's feelings about winning went far beyond a game in gym class.

Once in a while, Janie wished she could be Carla's friend. But most of the time, Janie just wanted to prove she could do something better. Now as she faced Carla, their gym teacher, Miss Macklin, held up the basketball.

"How you play is more important than winning," Mackey often said. "People are more important than points."

But Janie just wanted to win. As the whistle blew, she leaped high in the air, tipping the ball to her teammate Liz. Liz dribbled her way out of a tight spot and moved down the court. Janie slipped under the basket and waited for the ball. When it came she managed a jump shot.

Swish! It went in!

Janie's team, the Js, cheered, but Carla's team, the Cs, looked ready to fight every step of the way. It was their ball.

Standing at the end of the court, Carla looked around. When she spotted a break in the Js' defense, she threw the ball in. Her teammate caught it and headed toward the basket. Then the ball returned to Carla. Her long shot bounced on the board but dropped in.

Back and forth the score jumped with one side leading, then the other. At the half the score was tied, 24 to 24. Janie knew the game would be hard fought to the end. Facing Carla was always tough.

I'm just as good a player, Janie told herself. *But I always seem to lose.*

With only a few minutes left in the final quarter, the score was 40 to 38, the Js ahead. *If only we can keep it!* Janie ached with the desire to win.

Muscles tense, she guarded Carla closely. Swinging her arms up and down, Janie tried to block a pass to the Cs. Then, as Carla started in for a basket, Janie grabbed the ball.

The whistle blew. "Foul!"

Janie groaned. Carla moved to the free-throw line. Her first try fell short. Janie breathed deeply. But the second one dropped in. 40 to 39. Her team led by one point.

As the ball went into play, Janie's team caught it and started moving toward their own basket. Liz passed the ball to Janie. Carla leaped high and intercepted. In the same moment, she lost her footing and landed on the floor. The ball spun out of her hands.

Janie grabbed for it. Just before the ball rolled out of bounds, she touched it.

Mackey's whistle shrilled. "Js' ball!"

Janie looked back, surprised at the call. Had Carla's body blocked Mackey's view? Janie knew she didn't have the right to take the ball, but Mackey hadn't seen her touch it.

In that split second, Janie's thoughts jumped ahead. Having the ball now could make the difference between winning and losing. *Carla was on her back. She didn't see*, Janie told herself. *No one will ever know.*

As she picked up the basketball, Janie saw Carla look at her. For a split second Janie wondered if Carla knew. *If she did, she'd say something*, Janie told herself. *I can get by with it.*

She walked to the sideline, and Mackey joined her there. Janie waited for the whistle that would send the ball into play. *If my team can keep it one minute, we'll win*, she thought.

But as Janie stood there, she remembered Mackey's favorite saying: *"People are more important than points."*

Once more Janie debated with herself, unsure what to do. A knot formed in the pit of her stomach. *We're almost there*, she thought. *We can win. But what if we beat Carla, and I know it wasn't fair?*

Her feelings weren't in it, but Janie turned to Mackey. "I don't think I should have the ball. I touched it just before it went out."

Mackey looked surprised but signaled for Carla to take Janie's place. Carla threw the ball out, and everyone snapped into action. Janie kept close, but suddenly Carla broke loose. One of the Cs passed her the ball.

Instantly Carla took a long shot. Just as it went in, the final whistle blew. Final score was 40 to 41! The Cs had won the game.

Janie groaned. Her shoulders slumped. "By *one* point! By one point we lost!"

As soon as she could, Janie headed for the locker room and a bench in an out-of-the way corner. She didn't want to talk with anyone.

But her friend Liz found her there. "How come you told Mackey? We would have won."

Janie couldn't answer. She felt mad at herself. Mad for being honest. She had almost tasted victory, then she'd let it slip out of her hands.

"No one would have known," said Liz.

"I guess you're right," Janie answered out of her discouragement.

Just then she heard Carla's voice behind her. "I would have known," she said. "As I rolled over, I saw Janie touch the ball. I would have said something. I was waiting to see what she'd do."

As Janie turned she looked straight into Carla's eyes and felt glad that she could.

"You played a good game, Janie." Carla held out her hand.

Janie grasped it. "You played a good game, too." Janie felt surprised that she meant it.

Carla grinned. "When we start playing other schools, we'll be on the same team. I'll like that."

Seeing something new in Carla's eyes, Janie felt warm all the way though. *Maybe we'll even be friends.*

TO **TALK** ABOUT

▸ It was hard for Janie to be honest. Then she lost the game besides. Why is it important to be honest, even when things don't seem to turn out right?

▸ Sometimes it's easy to think, *Win, no matter what you have to do.* How would Janie feel if she had beaten Carla by cheating? How would it make her feel about having a friendship with Carla?

▸ If Janie had won the game by cheating, how would Carla

---

feel about being friends? Why?

▸ Have you ever had a friend who didn't tell the truth? Were you able to trust that friend? Why or why not? What happened to your friendship? Explain.

▸ **A person who is fair is a friend who cheers you on.** In what ways does Jesus cheer you on? See John 10:14, 27. In what ways has someone helped you by being fair and honest? In what ways have you helped someone else by being honest?

▸ Why do you think this story is called "The Real Winner"? Who really won in the end? In what way?

Even children show what they are by what they do; you can tell if they are honest and good. Proverbs 20:11 (TEV)

Jesus, I want to be someone people can count on. Help me to be honest and play fair. Help me do what's right, even when you're the only One who knows. Thank you!

Throwaway Friend

"Thanks, Dad," Heidi said as she climbed out of the car. Her best friend, Sara, said good-bye and followed Heidi.

Standing on the sidewalk, they looked up at the large SKATELAND sign. Both of them liked swooping along an outdoor path with their in-line skates, but with bad weather they needed to skate inside. All week they had looked forward to Saturday afternoon.

Minutes later Heidi and Sara tied the laces on their skates and stood up. It was still early, but the rink was filling up fast. As they moved into the flow of skaters, Heidi edged toward the middle. She wanted to practice some new turns before the rink got crowded.

She was beginning to feel good about her moves when she heard someone call her name. Looking up, she saw Annette, a girl from her class at school.

"Hey, this is gonna be great!" thought Heidi, waving back. Annette and her friends were the most popular kids in the class.

Last year Annette had been class president. She always managed to be in the middle of anything fun. Being Annette's friend was a sure ticket to being popular.

What can I do to have her pay attention to me? Heidi

---

wondered, then remembered how well she skated. *Maybe Annette will notice.*

She did. When the group skating stopped, Annette came over to where Heidi and Sara waited on the sidelines.

"You're a good skater, Heidi," said Annette, not seeming to notice Sara.

Just then a special skate was called. "Triples," said Annette to Heidi. "Why don't we ask Jon."

Heidi felt like she'd received an extra bonus. She'd had a secret crush on Jon for two years. *Skate with him?* she thought. *I'll jump at the chance!*

The afternoon began to seem like a once-in-a-lifetime dream. Annette or one of her friends got Heidi into each of the special skates. She barely noticed how often Sara sat on the sidelines.

When the manager announced, "Boy's choice," Jon skated up to Heidi. *Wow!* she thought. *He's really asking me!*

As they skated away, Heidi saw Sara's face. She seemed to have put on a mask, but for a moment the mask slipped. Sara's eyes looked hurt.

With a jolt, Heidi realized she'd been so busy with the other kids, she'd forgotten Sara. In fact, she hadn't brought her into a single skate.

As she and Jon moved away, Heidi once again forgot Sara. Jon was a good skater, and it was easy to keep in step. Soon they were laughing together. *He's as much fun as Sara,* thought Heidi.

In that moment a twinge of uneasiness shot through her. There it was again—Sara. Rounding a corner, Heidi saw her sitting on the bench by herself.

When the music ended, Heidi skated up to Sara. "Do you

want an ice cream?" she asked.

Acting as if nothing had come between them, her friend jumped up. And somehow Heidi found it a relief to be with Sara. *I don't have to impress her*, thought Heidi. *She's just what she always has been—my special friend.*

When they finished their ice cream, Heidi and Sara returned to the skating area. Again Heidi headed for the middle and started skating backward.

Annette found her there. "The kids are coming over to my house for supper," she said. "Want to come along?"

Do I want to! Heidi thought. *That isn't hard to decide.* She started to say yes, then remembered Sara.

"Sara and I came together. Can she come, too?"

A strange look crossed Annette's face. "Well, uh . . ."

For a moment she stood there, and Heidi guessed. Annette didn't want to say no, but she didn't want to say yes, either.

"Who's picking you up?" asked Annette.

"My dad," said Heidi.

"Why don't you take Sara home, then have your dad drop you off at my place."

Heidi was tempted. More than anything she wanted to go to Annette's. More than anything she wanted to be part of their group. But Heidi felt uneasy again. In that moment she knew what was wrong. *Am I throwing away Sara the minute someone else comes along?*

Heidi knew what her answer should be, but the world seemed to crash around her. *Will Annette ever invite me again?* She wished Annette hadn't forced her to make a choice.

But when Heidi spoke, she said, "I'm sorry. I'd like to come, but Sara's my friend."

Annette shrugged her shoulders and skated away. Heidi watched her go.

TO TALK ABOUT

▸ As you grow and change, your friends may change over time because you have different interests. How is that different from what happened between Heidi and Sara?

▸ In what ways would it seem good for Heidi to become friends with Annette? In what ways could it hurt Heidi to become friends with Annette? Give reasons for your answers.

▸ We live in a world of throwaways—soda cans, Styrofoam plates, plastic forks and spoons. What does it mean to have throwaway friends?

▸ What would happen to Heidi if she always chose her friends based on who seemed popular at the moment?

▸ How would Sara feel if she found out Heidi took her home, then went to Annette's? How would Heidi feel about herself if she did that to Sara?

▸ In the Bible we read about the friendship between David and Jonathan (1 Samuel 20). How was their friendship tested? Explain.

▸ What does the word *loyal* mean? How did Jonathan and David stay loyal to each other?

▸ Think about the friends you have. In what ways do you feel loyal to them? Are there ways they have been loyal to you?

▸ In Hebrews 13:5–6 there's a promise: **"God has said,**

'Never will I leave you; never will I forsake you.' So we say with confidence, 'The Lord is my helper; I will not be afraid. What can man do to me?' " Who will always be loyal to us? How do you know? In what ways can you give *your* loyalty?

Some friendships do not last, but some friends are more loyal than brothers. Proverbs 18:24 (TEV)

Jesus, you've given me some special friends. Help me to be loyal, so I don't throw away my friends whenever someone more popular comes around. Thanks for being my forever Friend. Most of all, I want to be loyal to you.

Dad's Marathon Run

"It's going to be cold, even for early October in Minnesota," Dad told Daniel as he talked about the marathon he planned to run the next day. "The weather people say it'll go down into the twenties tonight. Some of us could have trouble."

"What do you mean?" Daniel wanted to know.

"Running too hard, getting sweaty, then chilled. People can get hypothermia. In other words, really sick. Especially if we need to run into a cold wind."

For years Dad had been training for this day. Summer or winter, spring or fall, he ran after coming home from work. First he took short runs, then a thirteen-mile race on the snow of Lake Superior. Before that race Dad had said, *"If I can just finish, I'll feel like I've won."*

Dad had finished, all right. Daniel still remembered how proud he felt, watching Dad come across the finish line. And now the race was just over twenty-six miles long, starting in downtown Minneapolis, swinging around four lakes, crossing the Mississippi River, and finishing in downtown St. Paul.

"The real winners will be a couple hours ahead of me," Dad said, and again his goal was the same. "If I can just finish the race, I'll feel like I've won." But Dad had a second goal, too—running the race in four hours.

The day before the marathon, Daniel, his younger brother, Justin, and his six-year-old sister, Jennifer, piled into the car. Mom and Dad drove the route and figured out four places to stand along the way. Dad worked out a time sheet so the rest of them knew what time to be at what spot. And Mom knew exactly what to hand him each time he reached a checkpoint.

The morning of the marathon, Daniel went with Mom to drop Dad off at the beginning of the race. By eight o'clock Grandpa and Grandma met the rest of them at the house so all of them could.drive in one car.

The first checkpoint was five miles into the race next to Lake Harriet. Grandpa found parking close and easy. But along the route of the race, spectators lined the curb and crowded forward so Daniel couldn't see. One runner ran close to the people along the street, calling out, "Where are you, Katherine? Where are you?"

Listening to him, Daniel swallowed hard. What would it be like losing each other with seventy-five hundred people in the race?

When Dad found them and stopped for just a moment, Daniel felt relieved. Dad shed his jacket and kept running.

The second meeting place was on top of a hill. Before they reached it, Mom gave Daniel, Justin, and Jennifer cocoa and a second breakfast.

As Daniel watched the runners coming, officials pulled out a man who was having trouble. Then Daniel saw a number of women trying to qualify for the Olympics. After them came a man wearing red, orange, and yellow tights. In spite of the cold, another man ran without any shirt. And still another man was barefoot!

When Dad reached them, his hair was dripping wet, but he was still running strong.

Once again, Daniel and the others piled into the car. When Grandpa drove near the third checkpoint, barricades shut them off from the street Dad and Mom had planned to use. Grandpa wasn't able to park in a place close to the route of the race. For Daniel and the others, it meant a long walk.

But not as long as Dad's having to run, Daniel thought, but he was getting tired. So was his little sister, Jennifer. Now and then she ran ahead, and Mom had to call her back. By the time all of them found a place to stand, they weren't in the spot Dad expected to see Mom. Instead, they stood along the side of a steep uphill climb.

"Mile twenty-one," Mom told Grandma, and by now Daniel just wanted the race to be over. So did his brother, Justin, who started rolling around on the grass. Jennifer dropped down next to the street. Short and tiny, with long hair and a pixie face, she huddled on the curb. Holding her chin in her hands, she stared down the hill.

Even now some of the runners still looked strong. But some walked up the hill. A few looked as if every step hurt. One woman ran with her arm around another woman, encouraging her on.

Just then six-year-old Jennifer began calling out, "Keep on running! You're almost to the top. Keep on running! You're almost to the top!"

Half embarrassed, Daniel stared at his little sister. But Mom, Grandpa, and Grandma looked at Jennifer and grinned.

Then Daniel saw one of the runners glance toward Jennifer and smile. A few minutes later, another man looked her way. Holding up his hand in a high five of approval, he grinned.

For over twenty minutes Jennifer didn't let up. Never stopping once, she called out again and again, "Keep on running! You're almost to the top!"

Several more times a runner gave a thumbs-up, grinned, and kept on.

This time when Dad found them he was chilled and feeling pain in his back and toes. In the run along the river, he had felt a cold wind, and there were few people cheering. But now he, too, kept running up the hill.

Daniel and his family hurried back to the car and their final waiting place. As Dad neared the finish line, he headed down John Ireland Boulevard in a sprint, passing other runners. When he crossed the finish line, he was only five minutes over his goal.

Mom's excitement lit her face. Justin waved his arms, still cheering for Dad.

"He finished!" Daniel exclaimed. "Dad really finished!"

Turning, he grinned at his little sister, still able to hear her words: *"Keep on running! You're almost to the top!"*

At the family meeting place, Dad's smile was tired but real. To his family he was the best winner of all.

TO **TALK** ABOUT

▶ Sometimes we think that happiness is being number one in a race, even if it's number one out of seventy-five hundred runners. But in life, as in a marathon, what's most important is how we run a race. Daniel's dad had set goals for what he felt he could do. Did he meet those goals? Explain.

▶ What if Daniel and his family took the wrong road, missed the freeway exit, and couldn't find a parking place? What if they didn't see Dad actually finish? How would they feel? How would Dad feel?

▶ Was seeing the actual finish the most important thing? Or were the ways the family worked together the most important? How did Daniel and his family help Dad be a winner? In what ways did they need to work together?

▶ Dad won a medal for running 26.2 miles in a marathon. But what is the biggest medal any dad can win?

▶ Daniel and his family wanted to encourage Dad by being there—to cheer him on and give him hope. What are some ways you can give hope to other people? Here's a start:

- Saying, "I love you, Mom. I love you, Dad."
- Giving a welcome hug to Grandpa and Grandma when they come.
- Picking up newspapers thrown on the neighbor's lawn when they're gone on vacation.
- Telling your family the fun or funny things that happened during your day.
- Slipping surprise "love you" messages into Mom or Dad's suitcase if one of them travels for work.

Get the idea? See how long a list you can make. Write it down in the space below or on the next page. You might need much more room!

Let us run with determination the race that lies before us. Let us keep our eyes fixed on Jesus, on whom our faith depends from beginning to end. He did not give up because of the cross. Hebrews 12:1b–2a (TEV)

Jesus, when I want to give up because I think something is too hard to do, help me fix my eyes on you. You did not give up, but instead ran straight for the cross. Thank you that you will help me run the race of my life in a special way. Thank you for being my forever Friend. I love you,

Jesus!

You Are Loved!

Do you remember Kaitlin and Zachery and how they felt? They were thinking, *I want to be liked. I want people cheering for me. I want people to think I'm the greatest kid on earth.*

While reading these stories, you met kids who felt the same way. You made choices. Or you thought about ones you'd like to make.

Perhaps you also made a discovery. **Jesus loves you, whoever you are, whatever has happened to you. Whatever you face, you can count on Him.**

But there's a choice to make. Do you want to receive His help?

When you say YES! you live under God's protection. You let Him give you the power and the help you need.

Maybe you've discovered it's easier to trust Jesus when it's rough going. It's easier because you can no longer depend on yourself.

That's a good place to be.

That's when you learn to know God. And your relationship with Him is the most important relationship of all.

The book of Daniel says, "The people who know their

God shall be strong and do great things" (Daniel 11:32b, TLB).

Do you want to be strong in God? Do you want to do great things for Him? Not to make yourself look good, but because you love Him?

The great things of God happen when you choose, like Daniel, to put God first. Then your other relationships fall into place. Your friendships become real and lasting and fun.

Sometimes you may feel, *The choices are so hard I'm afraid to make any at all.* In those moments, ask Jesus to show you what to do. Then be willing to do it.

Other times you may think, *Oops! I goofed!* When that happens, be honest with Jesus. Tell Him about it. Then ask Him to help you turn your goofs into something good. All of us learn, not only by our good choices, but also through our poor ones.

The great things of God begin in small ways, with day-by-day choices. With each small choice you choose a habit you want to form. But your small choices also add up to help you make big ones.

So keep on making good choices in whatever you face each day. Keep on choosing friends who will help you grow strong. Keep on choosing to be a friend to your family and others.

Most of all, choose to know God. Choose to put Him first.

Jesus is cheering for you. He wants the best for you. He wants you to know, "I have called you friends . . . As the Father has loved me, so have I loved you. Now remain in my love" (John 15:15b and verse 9).

Remember? **Jesus stands with His arms wide open to you. He invites you to be His forever Friend.**

Acknowledgments

With gratitude to

Jesus Christ,
the center of my life
and
my most important relationship,

and warm thanks to these other valued people:

Judy Carter, Larry Hackett, Beverly Sandberg,
Jeffrey Johnson, and Kevin Johnson
for helpful information.

Jerry Foley, Charette Barta, Penny Stokes, and Terry White,
who offered the gift of wonderful critiques
and became my friends.

Traci Mullins, Rochelle Glöege,
Natasha Sperling, and Janna Anderson,
who combined excellent editing
with heartwarming encouragement.

My husband, Roy,
for the love, wisdom, and daily caring
out of which good relationships are built.

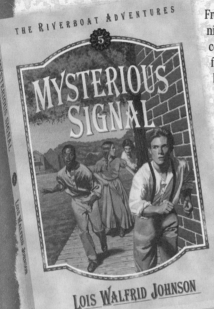